The Tower Rises: A Chronology

FLWF 5215.001 © Frank Lloyd Wright Foundation

1952

MAY 26

Harold C., Jr. and Joe Price, on the recommendation of Bruce Goff, suggest to their father Harold C. Price, Sr. to hire Frank Lloyd Wright as the architect for the future oil pipeline company headquarters. Wright invites the Prices for a visit to Taliesin, Wisconsin in June that year.[1]

JUNE 10

The building committee consisting of Harold C. Price, Sr., Mary Lou (Harold C. Price, Sr.'s wife), Harold C. Price, Jr., Joe Price, and one company officer arrive at Taliesin.

JUNE 16

Price, Sr. thanks Wright for the visit to Taliesin and mentions the H.C. Price Company is looking for an appropriate lot for a new building. The Price Company had to buy one from the Public Service Company of Oklahoma and trade it to get a larger lot that would host both companies. The Public Service Company will be the tenant for the ground and second floors of the new building.[2]

Harold Price and Frank Lloyd Wright look over the plans for the tower. Photograph by Joe Price (PTAC 2003.16.004).

1952

JULY 24

Elmer L. Gallery, treasurer for the H.C. Price Co., sends Wright the layout for the Public Service Company's Home Service Department, showing its minimum needs on the ground floor.[3]

AUGUST 19

Price, Sr. sends to Wright the summary of the requirements for the rest of the building, explaining: "When we first came to see you we had in mind that we would build a three or four story building, with 8,000 feet on each floor. You immediately convinced us that it would be more feasible to build higher, with smaller area on each floor, and that it would cost no more; therefore, we are now contemplating a building of no less than ten stories. We will need three stories ourselves, and the Public Service Company will need two or three…. With that in mind, the idea of including living apartments in the building was suggested. There is a demand in Bartlesville for what might be called deluxe apartments, that is, two bedrooms and two baths, one large-size living room with adjacent dinette and kitchen."[4]

SEPTEMBER 16

Four weeks after the program is established, Wright finishes the preliminary sketches[5] and invites Price, Sr. to see the plans at Taliesin, Wisconsin.[6]

OCTOBER 27

Price, Sr. contemplates the possibility of adding two more floors to the tower depending on the number of tenants.[7]

Letter from Frank Lloyd Wright to Harold C. Price, Sr. stating the publications' interest in the Price Tower (PTAC 2004.02.08).

NOVEMBER 4

Wright completes the sketches of the inside views of a typical office, a typical apartment, and designs for Price, Sr.'s office and furniture.[8]

DECEMBER 11

NBC's television series "Famous Americans" chooses the Price Tower to be the ending of a program on Frank Lloyd Wright. Also, the *Architectural Forum* and part of the Luce publications (*Life* and *Time*) are interested in publishing articles on the Price Tower.[9]

1953

JANUARY 2

Price, Sr. is reluctant to show the Price Tower designs on television prior to their distribution in the Luce publications.[10]

MARCH 12

Price, Sr. asks Wright to complete drawings soon in order to get estimates from contractors; he also wants a color picture on the cover of the next issue of *The Tie-In*, the Price company publication.[11]

PRICE TOWER ARTS CENTER ■

RIZZOLI NEW YORK

PRAIRIE
Frank Lloyd Wright's

APRIL 2

Price, Sr. wants to arrange publicity, including the estimated building cost, before the model is shown at the International Petroleum Exposition in Tulsa.[12]

APRIL 6

Price, Sr. asks Wright to travel to Bartlesville with the plans to meet with potential contractors.[13]

APRIL 17

Wright sends the plans with William Wesley Peters, upset with Harold C. Price, Sr. for inviting six bidders instead of two or three at most.[14]

APRIL 18

Wright sends Price, Sr. the script for an article on the Price Tower for the *Architectural Forum*.[15] The text (dated 4.17.1953) describes the tower's advantages: casting its shadow upon its own ground rather than on other buildings; hastening decentralization by becoming an agent of desirable concentration; and having a design based on a compact quadrant composition housing duplex residence apartments and office spaces with absolute privacy between quadrants and unobstructed views. For Wright, the tower develops its full expression based on its isolation and free standing position in the countryside. "Witness this release of the skyscraper from slavery (commercial bondage) to humane freedom,"[16] concludes Wright.

SKYSCRAPER
Price Tower

Anthony Alofsin, editor

WITH ESSAYS BY
Anthony Alofsin
Joseph M. Siry
Pat Kirkham and Scott W. Perkins
Hilary Ballon

AND CONTRIBUTIONS BY
Mónica Ramírez-Montagut
Richard P. Townsend

APRIL 20	APRIL 30	MAY 14	JUNE 4
The contractors submitting final bids are Manhattan Construction Company of Muskogee, OK; W. R. Grimshaw Company of Tulsa, OK; Culwell Construction Company of Oklahoma City, OK; Harmon Construction Company of Oklahoma City, OK; and Long Construction Company of Kansas City, MO.[17]	The construction companies' estimates are presented to Price, Sr. who feels they are too high.[18]	The model of the Price Tower is unveiled at the International Petroleum Exposition in Tulsa, OK.[20]	Wright is concerned about a construction cost published in the *Architectural Forum* article that he considers erroneous. He suggests working only with one contractor, and most likely Culwell.[22]
	MAY 11 Price, Sr. sends Wright a sample of the gold tinted glass, known as "golden polished plate glass" proposed for the building.[19]	**MAY 19** Clean up of the site starts, and licenses for construction are being formalized.[21]	

Price Tower scale model at the New York Usonian
Exhibition Pavilion. © Pedro E. Guerrero.

First published in the United States of America in 2005 by
RIZZOLI INTERNATIONAL PUBLICATIONS, INC.
in conjunction with the exhibition *Prairie Skyscraper: Frank Lloyd Wright's Price Tower* organized by Price Tower Arts Center, Bartlesville, Oklahoma, in cooperation with The Frank Lloyd Wright Foundation, Scottsdale, Arizona. The exhibition, its tour and publication are made possible in part by the Henry Luce Foundation, the Buell Family of Bartlesville, and the Oklahoma Tourism and Recreation Department. *Prairie Skyscraper* has been curated by Anthony Alofsin with the assistance of Mónica Ramírez-Montagut. The exhibition installation has been designed by Zaha Hadid and Office of Zaha Hadid, London, and co-produced by Price Tower Arts Center and Yale University Art + Architecture Gallery.

Price Tower Arts Center
Bartlesville, Oklahoma
14 October 2005 – 15 January 2006

Yale University Art + Architecture Gallery
New Haven, Connecticut
13 February – 5 May 2006

National Building Museum
Washington, D.C.
17 June – 17 September 2006

Catalogue design: Dung Ngo/NGOstudio.com & Martine Trelaun/savoir-faire.org
Photography: Joe Price, Steven Brooke Studios, Christian M Korab/Korab Photo, and Amatucci Photography.

ISBN: 0-8478-2754-2 (HC)
ISBN: 0-8478-2788-7 (PB)
LCCN: 2005924723

2005 2006 2007 2008 2009 / 10 9 8 7 6 5 4 3 2 1

Rizzoli International Publications, Inc.
300 Park Avenue South
New York, New York 10010
www.rizzoliusa.com

Price Tower Arts Center
510 Dewey Avenue
Bartlesville, OK 74003
www.pricetower.org

1953

JUNE 5

Price, Sr. doubts the article in the *Forum* will have any effect on the actual cost of the building. He has selected two contractors: Culwell and Long. He leaves to Wright the decision of which to hire. Price, Sr. mentions to Wright: "We now have the challenge of refuting FORUM'S statement by erecting the building at a cost in line with your original estimate."[23]

JUNE 8

Price, Sr. asks Wright if he could borrow the Price Tower model and exhibit it at the Elks National Convention in St. Louis, MO, although he doubts it will be available since the model is on exhibit in the New York Usonian Exhibition Pavilion, NYC (on the site where the Guggenheim Museum would be built three years later).[24]

JUNE 20

H.C.Price Company, Culwell Construction Company, and Frank Lloyd Wright draft the construction contract and agree on the cost of the building at $1,250,000.

JULY 4

The electrical and structural plans for pavements, flower boxes, carport columns, tower shafts, mezzanine level, typical main floors, interior partitions, doors, stairways, and glazing schedules are done.[25]

JULY 13

Wright modifies the materials of the façades of the building to bring down costs.[26]

JULY 14	JULY 30	NOVEMBER 10
Wright considers the gas connections and service requirements for the Gas Service Company of Oklahoma.[27]	George E. Thompson Co. provides the specifications of the lightning protection equipment for Wright's consideration.[29]	**Price Tower's construction begins.**

NOVEMBER 14
400 additional square feet are excavated under the auditorium wing so that the basement rests on bedrock.[32]

JULY 22
Air supply units are calculated by Samuel R. Lewis and Associates and submitted for Wright's approval. [28]

AUGUST 24
Wright revises structural plans for the basement and footings, and revises electrical plans.[30]

OCTOBER 12
Wright revises structural plans for upper floors and elevations.[31]

The State of Oklahoma
Office of the Governor

Fifty years ago, the completion of Frank Lloyd Wright's Price Tower moved a visionary architect another step forward in his ambition to change the way people use and experience buildings. With this publication and exhibition, Oklahoma celebrates one of our state's greatest treasures and shares its story with the world.

Wright's integration of beauty, art, and innovation in everyday places has indeed influenced our perception of the buildings around us. Many people throughout the years have been inspired by the Price Tower's dynamic spaces and sculptural form. Today this magnificent structure has become a beacon of architectural enlightenment, sharing the world of architecture and Wright's vision with people from around the globe.

As intended, the Price Tower's design and spirit have proven timeless. Wright created the high-rise to be a multi-use building, bringing together commercial offices, retail stores and apartments. Even when changing times led to a single occupant for the building, it continued to serve multiple functions, providing education, enlightenment and a historical record through the efforts of Price Tower Arts Center and Phillips Petroleum Company. Now those roles have been expanded, and it has been returned to a multi-use building in the spirit of Wright's original vision.

Since the tower's recent rehabilitation, Price Tower Arts Center has made it possible for the public to immerse themselves in this masterpiece, whether through its stunning hotel, fine dining or guided tours. The organization also presents art, architecture and design exhibitions as well as educational programs for local, regional and global audiences. Through this fiftieth anniversary project, the Arts Center provides the first critical examination of Price Tower and presents it across the country at Yale University and the National Building Museum

Oklahoma is fortunate that Harold C. Price, Sr. embraced such a progressive vision and Mr. Wright accepted the invitation to bring his genius to Bartlesville. We are proud to share one of his most important creations with the world.

Governor Brad Henry

1954

JANUARY 7

Wright visits Bartlesville when the building is barely above the ground.[33]

JANUARY 18
Joe Price is working on a script for a Hollywood movie about Wright and the tower: "The scene is now written to begin with space (the open rolling hills of the prairie), followed by nature and then the relationship of both of these to the skyscraper."[34]

JANUARY 25

William Wesley Peters, from the office of Frank Lloyd Wright, writes to Haskell Culwell, from the construction company, and gives Wright's specifications on stair rails and all door hardware, the shade of red for the floor medallion, the lobby and main entrance, the drainage of planting areas over carport, the apartment kitchen, the bus-duct, the heating grilles, and the light fixtures layout. Wright also revises the plans for the basement and footings.[35]

FEBRUARY 24
A metalworker's strike halts construction.[36]

MARCH 13

The strike is over,[37] and Harold C. Price, Jr. estimates ten weeks of construction time lost.[38]

APRIL 12
Furniture specifications are underway and ready for the manufacturer.[39]

Price Tower with the nineteenth floor finished.
Photograph by Joe Price (PTAC 2003.16.068).

Price Tower as the twelfth floor is being poured. Photograph by Joe Price (PTAC 2003.16.054).

MAY 17

Haskell Culwell asks Wright's approval on the specifications of materials and colors for the Otis elevators.[40]

AUGUST 26
Wright sends the furniture layout plans for office, apartments, dentist, and gynecologist to Price, Sr., Haskell Culwell, and Joe Price.[41]

OCTOBER 1

Haskell Culwell sends to the Industrial Electric Company the drawing from Westinghouse Electric approved by Wright.[42]

OCTOBER 22
The twelfth floor of the building is poured towards the end of October.[43]

DECEMBER 4
Frank Lloyd Wright plans to visit Bartlesville in late December.[44]

1955

JANUARY 15

Construction of the nineteenth floor is underway.[45]

FEBRUARY 14
Windows and doors are being installed.[46]

Price Tower Casual Chair. Cast aluminum frame with orange re-upholstery. PTAC 2001.01.003. (Catalogue No. 48). Photograph by Steven Brooke Studios, 2004.

1955

APRIL 12

Wright determines an aluminum mold edge for all furniture and sends specifications for Price, Sr.'s desk, caretaker's dining room table, ventilation in ceilings, light needle on top of tower, and dishwasher installation in the apartment kitchens.[47]

MAY 25

Price, Sr. wishes some changes be made to the design of the Stenographer chair, Clerk's chair, Executive chair, and Guest chair. The manufacturer at that time is Do/More Chair Company in Elkhart, Indiana.[48] Eventually, the manufacturer will be Blue Stem Foundry in Dewey, Oklahoma.

JUNE 5

Under Wright's specifications and Mary Lou Price's coordination, one apartment is furnished in order to sell the others.[49]

JUNE 7

Wright plans to visit Bartlesville to talk with Joe Price about the movie on the tower.[50]

JUNE 22

Price, Sr. wishes more modifications to be made to the chairs and is concerned about opening the building without furniture.[51]

AUGUST 10

Hassocks (ottomans) have been completed as designed and approved.[52]

Price Tower with apartment vertical louvers installed halfway down. Photograph by Joe Price (PTAC 2003.16.116).

AUGUST 20

Price, Sr. asks Wright to urgently visit Bartlesville and decide on many structural problems, to which the architect replies that unless the building is falling down, he knows of no such emergencies.[53]

SEPTEMBER 2
Wright reviews the final specifications for the desks and chairs.[54]

SEPTEMBER 21

Joe Price sends Eugene Masselink the film titled *The Toughest Inch* on pipeline construction to inspire him for Harold C. Price, Sr.'s office mural.[55] The louvers of the building are halfway down on the apartments on the north side. The furnishing of one of the apartments has started.[56] Joe Price explains: "Frank Lloyd Wright envisioned the tower as a tree first growing upwards and then flourishing downwards, dressing up the building."[57]

SEPTEMBER 30
Architectural Record is interested in publishing an article on the Price Tower for the February 1956 issue.[58]

FOREWORD

This story—that of arguably America's greatest and most loved architect and the Oklahoma industrialist who together caused to rise from the prairie a singular skyscraper—is nothing short of riveting. As compelling is the story of how this landmark has since developed into a cultural destination like few others, a proud civic symbol of the city that oil built brought wholly back to life by dedicated members of its community. Herein you will find the story related as never before. Marking the 50th anniversary of the completion and opening of Price Tower in 1956, *Prairie Skyscraper: Frank Lloyd Wright's Price Tower* has provided the occasion for much work, most notably this first comprehensive critical analysis of Wright's landmark. It is also the first publication devoted to the building since Frank Lloyd Wright's own account, *The Story of the Tower* (1956). In preparation, we have acquired significant objects for the permanent collection related to the exhibition, transferred original documentary construction film footage to digital format, and are publishing and exhibiting many drawings, photographs, films, and other documentation for the very first time. This is simultaneous with our efforts to conserve and restore the original extant Wright interiors (on the executive floors 17-19) to their former glory, which we hope to unveil within the next few years.

As Price Tower Arts Center may be unfamiliar to some, it is appropriate to say a few words about it at this juncture. The Arts Center's mission is to offer a singular experience in art, architecture and design, exploring the intersection of these disciplines through our exhibitions (especially of contemporary art), our nascent architecture study center, and the preservation and interpretation of this landmark structure. Our socially entrepreneurial Inn at Price Tower, a 21 room high-design hotel and restaurant designed by Wendy Evans Joseph within Wright's skyscraper, provides an immersion experience in architecture and design of the past and present. Price Tower Arts Center—originally incorporated in 1985 as a civic art museum—was reorganized in 1998 as it began to more tightly focus its mission. In addition to the rapidly growing collections of architecture, design and contemporary art (with a significant focus on Frank Lloyd Wright and Bruce Goff), Bartlesville itself is home to important buildings by Welton Becket, Edward Buehler Delk, John Duncan Forsyth, Bruce Goff, Clifford May, William Wesley Peters, and Frank Lloyd Wright, forming an impressive survey of aspects of 20th century American architecture. To accommodate our growing collections and programs, we commissioned several years ago the design for a new museum facility to adjoin Price Tower from Pritzker Prize laureate Zaha Hadid, which when combined with these other components, will comprise an unparalleled architectural destination.

It is my distinct pleasure to acknowledge a number of people without whom there would be no Price Tower, much less a Price Tower Arts Center. Most notably they are Harold C. Price, Jr., Joe D. Price, and Carolyn S. Price. We owe them and Harold and Joe's parents, Harold Senior and Mary Lou Price, our gratitude for their collective act of courage and vision in helping realize Frank Lloyd Wright's long-awaited dream to build his utopian skyscraper. I thank Harold and his wife Sandy for their ongoing support, Joe and Etsuko Price for their great generosity in devel-

1955

NOVEMBER 16

The Cigar Stand on the first floor is being constructed.[59]

NOVEMBER 18

The carports have been planted and Joe Price has finished the photography for the book *The Story of the Tower*.[60]

DECEMBER 21

Spinning Wheel Rugs sends four rugs for installation in Price, Sr.'s office, the apartment living room and two bedrooms.[61]

DECEMBER 22

Price's office is finished with exception of the glass mural.[62]

DECEMBER 27

As the opening of the building approaches, Price, Sr. asks Wright to finish defining the details for the entrance, Executive chair, fireplace, air-conditioning, sidewalks, door handles, and mail box, among other items.[63]

DECEMBER 28

Wright designs the car stops for the parking spaces.[64]

oping our collections, and Carolyn Price for her kindness, counsel and volunteer service to the Arts Center. Likewise, it is most appropriate to recognize here the instrumental role that C.J. "Pete" and his wife Theo Silas have played in the development of Price Tower Arts Center. Without their generous support, the Arts Center could not have developed as it has. ConocoPhillips (formerly Phillips Petroleum Company), which Pete Silas ably guided for many years, gave us in 2001 the building, its contents and renovation, representing an extraordinary act of corporate philanthropy. We dedicate this effort to those above with deepest gratitude.

This definitive study on Wright's Price Tower was largely made possible by Joy and Barry Buell, in memory of his mother Bernice, and the Henry Luce Foundation, New York. We thank them for their support. The exhibition and its accompanying catalogue provide yet another example of the Luce Foundation's leadership role in the study of American art and architecture, and I thank in particular Michael Gilligan, President, and Ellen Holtzman, Program Director. We are also grateful to the National Endowment for the Humanities and the National Endowment for the Arts for their assistance. It is an honor to have the State of Oklahoma assist in making possible *Prairie Skyscraper*'s national tour. We thank the Honorable Brad Henry, Governor of Oklahoma, Deputy Press Secretary Lu Eyerman and the Department of Tourism and Recreation, especially Robb Gray, Executive Director, and Hardy Watkins, Deputy Director, for their support.

Many dedicated persons have worked on this project. First of all, we are indebted to Prof. Anthony Alofsin, not only for his pioneering work in Wright studies, but for serving as guest curator and editor for *Prairie Skyscraper*. His colleagues Hilary Ballon, Pat Kirkham, Scott W. Perkins, and Joseph Siry have provided insightful essays on various aspects of the Price Tower. The publication itself is the result of the tasteful and concise design of Dung Ngo and the good offices of David Morton, Senior Editor, Rizzoli, to both of whom we are grateful. The exhibition design is by Zaha Hadid and Office of Zaha Hadid, London. We deeply thank Zaha, Woody Yao and Ana Cajiao for their work.

At the Arts Center, Mónica Ramírez-Montagut, Curator of Collections and Public Programs, has skillfully coordinated this effort and contributed the extremely useful construction chronology and exhibition catalogue. Kay Johnson, Registrar, has been of tremendous service in organizing the exhibition and its tour. We are thankful for the assistance of Bruce Brooks Pfeiffer and Margo Stipe of the Frank Lloyd Wright Foundation Archives, Scottsdale, Arizona. Finally, I would like to thank our former curator Kara J. Hurst for early on helping launch the project.

It is our pleasure to send this exhibition across the country to audiences in our nation's capital and the Northeast. I thank Chase Rynd, Director, National Building Museum, Washington, D.C. and Robert Stern, Dean, and Dean Sakamoto, Gallery Director, School of Architecture, Yale University, for joining us to bring one of the great buildings by America's greatest architect in its 50th anniversary year to a broader public.

Richard P. Townsend
Executive Director and CEO
Price Tower Arts Center

JANUARY 2

The H.C. Price Co. moves into the Tower. A Walt Whitman quote is painted in gold on the wall of the main entry: "Toward all I raise high the perpendicular hand, I make the signal to remain after me in sight forever, for all the haunts and homes of men. Where the city of the faithfullest friends stands, where thrift is in its place but prudence is in its place, where behavior is the finest of the fine arts, where outside authority enters always after the precedence of inside authority, where the city that has produced the greatest man stands, there the greatest city stands."[65]

JANUARY 19
A masseuse will have offices in the northeast quadrant of the third floor.[66]

FEBRUARY 4

Wright redistributes the parking based on the changes of the sizes of new cars: "four years ago when we laid out parking, cars were not what they are now. The cars are now bigger and square with the corners emphasized… square moving platforms." He assigns the two courts-stalls for officials to avoid crowding at the main entrance to the building. Visitors and employees will drive in and out through the tunnel to go to the parking area at the rear.[67]

Crowds waiting in line to visit Price Tower on opening day. Photograph by Joe Price (PTAC 2003.16.232).

FEBRUARY 9

FEBRUARY 18

FEBRUARY 22

FEBRUARY 23

1956

Price Tower's construction finished.

The H.C. Price Company announces on February 9, 1956 the Tower will be open for three days of public inspection immediately following the dedication ceremonies at 10 am Friday, February 10. The days for public tours are February 10, 11, and 12 until 9:00pm.[68]

An article in the national magazine *Business Week* states the Price Tower was a bad investment where the Price employees are "victimized by the impractical." Wright replies with the intention of suing the magazine for $250,000 on his behalf and for $500,000 on Price, Sr.'s behalf for damages to reputation and investment.[69]

Wright feels the dedication of the tower was a success and explains "the show has just begun and will go on for years and years."[70]

Price, Sr. writes to *Business Week* stating that "there is consistently an attitude of criticism of Mr. Wright's architecture, based only on minor defects such as leaky windows and unbalanced chairs. There is no mention of the outstanding beauty and efficiency of the design...."[71]

Mr. Harold C. Price
The Price Tower
Bartlesville

Dear Hal: This will introduce to you Charles Glore
an earnest young client of mine at Lake Forest. He
is bringing a prominent Chicago contractor with him to
see our building. I hope you afford them -- the
breaks.

We miss you.

TALIESIN   Affectionately,
                Frank Lloyd Wright

                    July 2nd, 1956

Letter from Frank Lloyd Wright to Harold C. Price, Sr.
(PTAC 2004.02.60).

Frank Lloyd Wright and Harold C. Price, Sr. dedicate the new building, February 9, 1956. Photograph by Joe Price
(PTAC 2003.16.235).

MAY 3

In an interview Frank Lloyd Wright compares the other corporate buildings in Bartlesville, which he calls ugly boxes, to the Price Tower that graces the Prices' own town: "Why not take the skyscraper, make an ideal thing of it, plant it there as beautiful as a tree, and enjoy it yourselves." K.S. Adams, Chairman of Phillips Petroleum sends a copy of the interview to Price, Sr. asking him how many floors the size of the Price Tower would they need to house their entire organization.[72] Price, Sr. replies they would need 190 floors and expresses his regret at being "within range of Frank Lloyd Wright's verbal arrows. Never a dull moment."[73]

MAY 4

Harold C. Price, Sr. writes to Frank Lloyd Wright and reminds him: "Phillips may want to build a building some day, and I may need a pipeline from them to pay for the one I've got."[74]

JUNE 8

The Prices visit Frank Lloyd Wright at Taliesin, Spring Green for his birthday.[75]

JULY 2

Wright writes to Price, Sr., making a point of emphasizing the address as "The Price Tower" in red ink.[76]

DECEMBER 11

The Museum of Modern Art in New York is planning an exhibition on the Price Tower.[77]

ACKNOWLEDGMENTS

The Price Tower in Bartlesville, Oklahoma, is one of many tall buildings Frank Lloyd Wright designed during his long and creative career, but it is the only built example to represent his ideals. Completed fifty years ago, the Price Tower deserves both an exhibition and the accompanying book. Thus, the book begins with a general overview and introduction to the building. Joseph Siry's essay follows with a study in depth of Wright and the patronage of the Price family. Pat Kirkham and Scott W. Perkins then explore Wright's approach to total design and his coordination of objects, furnishings, and textiles to create a total work of art. Hilary Ballon contributes with a look at the transit from his prototype for the city to its realization in the country.

At Price Tower Arts Center, we wish to thank Richard P. Townsend, Executive Director and CEO; Kay Johnson, Registrar; Deshane Atkins, Curatorial Assistant; Elaine Bristol, Executive Assistant; John Womack, who provided in-depth research on the interiors; and Kara Hurst, former curator. At the Skyscraper Museum in New York City we thank Carol Willis, director and founder, and the staff, particularly Ned Dodington. Margo Stipe, Oscar Muñoz, and Bruce Brooks Pfeiffer at the Frank Lloyd Foundation were most helpful. We thank Pedro E. Guerrero, Dixie Legler, and George M. Goodwin. Finally, many at the University of Texas contributed, including Edgar Bocanegra, Cory Boden, Barbara Brown, Rina Faletti, Ricardo Ikeda, Alvaro Carrizosa, and Chad Lee.

We also wish to thank Harold C. Price, Jr.; Joe D. Price; Carolyn Price; Bill Creel; Jenny L. Brown, ConocoPhillips Corporate Archives, Bartlesville; the Bartlesville Public Library; Karen Smith Woods, Bartlesville Area History Museum; Professor Susanne Fusso, Wesleyan University; Rebecca Brave; Sue Lacey; Kate Holliday; and Otto Antonia Graf.

Finally, we are grateful to those who came before—the Landmark Preservation Council and The Bartlesville Museum and Sculpture Garden—for their setting high standards to which the Arts Center today aspires. We thank the Arts Center's hardworking staff and commend the efforts of its docents and volunteers.

Anthony Alofsin
Roland Roessner Centennial Professor
School of Architecture
The University of Texas at Austin

Mónica Ramírez-Montagut
Curator of Collections and Public Programs
Price Tower Arts Center

1956

DECEMBER 17

Eugene Smith wishes to photograph Price Tower for the American Institute of Architects Centennial Exhibition at the National Gallery of Art in Washington D.C.[78]

1957–2006

MARCH 21 1957

The Price Tower is causing "a tremendous impression on many people and even though it was not so intended it is coming to be an ever greater attraction to travelers,"[79] explains Henry Bass, one of the five contractors invited to submit a proposal for building Price Tower, in a letter to Price, Sr.

JANUARY 27 1959

Olgivanna Wright invites Price, Sr. and Mary Lou Price to join them for Wright's birthday at Taliesin on June 8.[80]

MARCH 16 1959
Frank Lloyd Wright dies.

JANUARY 28 1962
Harold C. Price, Sr. dies.

Photograph by Christian M Korab / Korab Photo, 2004.

1974

The National Register of Historic Places lists the Price Tower.[81]

1978
Mary Lou Price dies.

1981
The H. C. Price Company relocates to Dallas, Texas and Phillips Petroleum Company purchases the Price Tower.[82]

1983

The Price Tower wins the American Institute of Architects' prestigious Twenty-Five Year Award recognizing architectural design of enduring significance. The award is conferred on projects that have withstood the test of time for at least 25 years: "It can truly be said that the building use has not been altered from the original intent."[83]

1986
Phillips Petroleum Company invites the Landmark Preservation Council of Washington County, OK, to assume the docent duties for the tours of the Price Tower.[84]

1990

Phillips Petroleum Company makes space available in the Price Tower for the Bartlesville Museum. It opens with its first exhibition: "The Tree that Escaped the Crowded Forest, Frank Lloyd Wright and the Price Tower."[85]

Photographs by Christian M Korab/Korab Photo, 2004.

1957–2006

1998

The Bartlesville Museum is reorganized as Price Tower Arts Center.

2000

Phillips Petroleum Company refurbishes the Price Tower.[86]

2001

Phillips Petroleum Company donates the Price Tower to Price Tower Arts Center, under the leadership of C.J. Silas, former Phillips Chairman.

2002-2003

Price Tower Arts Center remodels eight floors of the tower into 21 high-design hotel rooms and a restaurant and bar (Inn at Price Tower and Copper). New York-based architect Wendy Evans Joseph designs the intervention, updating some of Wright's original architectural intentions.

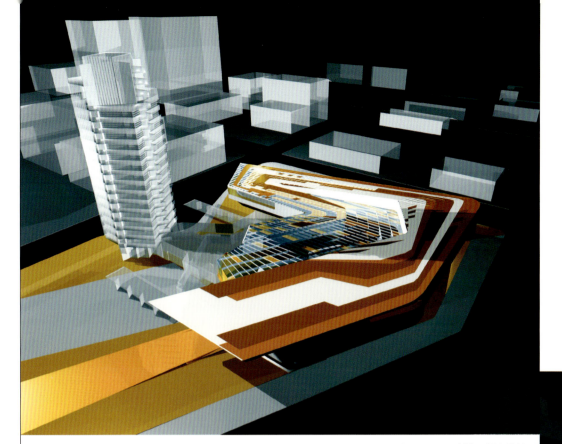

Images courtesy of Office of Zaha Hadid.

002

Pritzker Prize laureate Zaha Hadid is selected as architect of Price Tower Arts Center's new museum facility.

2006

50th anniversary of the completion of the tower.

The Tower Rises: A Chronology

by Mónica Ramírez-Montagut
Notes on page 172

PINWHEEL ON THE PRAIRIE: AN OVERVIEW OF THE PRICE TOWER

Anthony Alofsin

The Price Tower stands fifty years after its completion as a testament to Frank Lloyd Wright's system of design, uniting structure, ornament, and purpose into an organic whole. The Tower was the fulfillment of his dream to build a skyscraper in the American landscape. Though Wright designed several tall buildings during his long career, only two were erected: the Price Tower (1952–1956), headquarters for the H.C. Price Company; and the Johnson Wax Company Research Tower (1943–50), adjacent to the famous administration building in Racine, Wisconsin.[1] The Johnson Wax Research Tower has the "taproot" construction that fascinated Wright, but its height of 153 feet in fifteen stories, its limited use, and small size of 1,260 square feet per floor do not produce a building of the grand scale usually associated with skyscrapers (even though high-rise buildings are generally considered buildings of twelve stories). However, the Price Tower, despite its small footprint, fits very much into the American tradition of iconic, singular statements about tall buildings engaging the skyline and providing for the needs of business and dwelling (Fig. 1.1).

The most striking aspect of the Price Tower is its dramatic pinwheel geometry with shifting facades, unconventional base, and articulated top. A complex and elusive geometry informs every aspect of the building including floor plans, construction details, furniture, fabrics, and the murals that decorate its walls. This underlying geometry ties all the parts of the building into a harmonious, integrated whole; it is a total work of art in the spirit of *Gesamtkunstwerk* that drove Wright's designs from their beginnings in the 1890s to the last works in the late 1950s. Wright refined his earliest geometric experiments over decades of practice and experimentation. The Price Tower, coming near the end of Wright's fertile career, demonstrated how he used his organic system of geometry to build a skyscraper with a central supporting core and cantilevered floors. Looking closely at the evolution of this geometric language and its expression in the Price Tower reveals a symbolic function of the design that went beyond the traditional statements of corporate and economic power associated with tall buildings.

Rotational Geometry and Primary Forms

The role of geometry in Wright's designs is so fundamental and pervasive that it appears daunting to understand. But it is graspable if we proceed systematically and realize that there exists a great deal of continuity in his design methods across his career. From his earliest reliance on grids and squares, and through his later use of increasingly complex geometric matrices, circles, and triangles, Wright consistently relied on a complete system of geometry and proportion to create each design, from its floor plans and construction details to its elevations and ornament. He often rotated these shapes and his grids to create striking effects that emphasized diagonal visual forces. He carried this design method consistently into every phase of his work and into every project, whether for a building, furniture, or decorative object, and it allowed the dynamism of his spaces to emerge.

A long lineage of Wright's use of rectilinear geometry characterizes the compositional methods that ultimately articulate Price Tower. We can see the approach used throughout his early Prairie period from 1900 to 1910 embodied in the simple design of a detail for the Larkin Company Administration Building, Buffalo, New York (1903)(Fig. 1.2).[2] Abstracting his forms and using symmetrical arrangements, Wright employed the compositional motif of a square laid out on a grid, which he contrasted with symmetrically arranged diagonal elements. Symmetry kept

FOOTNOTES

1 For a selection of primary publications on the Price Tower and Wright's ideas about tall buildings, see the Selected Bibliography in this volume. Also of note are Frank Lloyd Wright, **The Future of Architecture** (New York: Horizon Press, 1953) and **A Testament Frank Lloyd Wright** (New York: Horizon Press, 1957). See also David G. De Long, ed., **Frank Lloyd Wright and the Living City** (Weil am Rhein, Germany: Vitra Design Museum, 1998); Idem., **Bruce Goff: Toward Absolute Architecture** (New York: Architecture History Foundation; and Cambridge, Mass.: MIT Press, 1988); and "Frank Lloyd Wright: The Vertical Dimension," whole issue, **Frank Lloyd Wright Quarterly** 15:3 (Summer 2004). A synopsis of Wright's tall buildings took place in the exhibition, *Frank Lloyd Wright: The Vertical Dimension*, Hilary Ballon, guest curator, and held at the Skyscraper Museum, New York, NY, from 6 October 2004 through 9 January 2005.

2 Cat. 1, FLWF 0403.166 includes the notation "STONE DIAGRAM," but the design is nearly identical to the model Wright used for a terrace-cotta pier capital at the Larkin Building. See Jack Quinan, **Frank Lloyd Wright's Larkin Building, Myth and Fact** (New York: Architectural History Foundation; and Cambridge, Mass.: MIT Press, 1987), 91, 92, fig. 94.

Figure 1.1 View of the Price Tower at dusk. Photograph by Steven Brooke Studios, 2004.

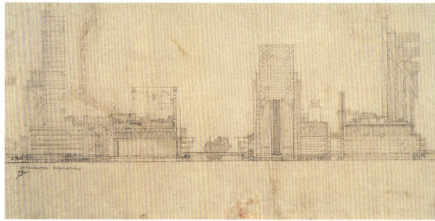

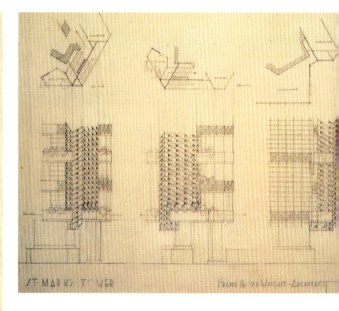

Figure 1.6 (Catalogue No. 6). National Life Insurance Building, Chicago, 1924 (project). Exterior perspective of the 24-story building. FLWF 2404.001. © Frank Lloyd Wright Foundation.

Figure 1.7 (Catalogue No. 7). Skyscraper regulation, 1926 (project). Urban development elevation. FLWF 2603.001. © Frank Lloyd Wright Foundation.

Figure 1.8 (Catalogue No. 9). St. Marks-in-the-Bouwerie, New York City 1929 (project). Exterior perspective view of the towers. FLWF 2905.028. © Frank Lloyd Wright Foundation.

Figure 1.9 (Catalogue No. 12). St. Marks-in-the-Bouwerie, New York City 1929 (project).Copper sheets placement. FLWF 2905.044. © Frank Lloyd Wright Foundation.

ed by their patterns.[6] Wright imagined that the Textile Block system would have much wider usage in terms of building types and locations, and, in a significant change to his design methods, he transferred the process of creating individual block designs to creating entire floor plans. This produced dramatic new diagonal configurations in a series of projects for houses, complexes, and resorts in California and the Southwest, of which almost none were built, including the A. M. Johnson Desert Compound (1924) and San Marcos in the Desert (1928).[7] Dynamic diagonal compositions added a fundamental tool to Wright's design methods that he applied to his long-standing interest in producing new types of skyscrapers.

Wright and the Tall Office Building
After working in the office of Louis Sullivan and Dankmar Adler in the 1890s and surrounded in Chicago by a great agglomeration of skyscrapers, Wright was naturally interested in this innovative American building type. He designed numerous tall buildings and skyscrapers throughout his career, but among the early works his project in 1912 for the newspaper, the *San Francisco Call*, was his most important. Conceived as a highly contextual urban gesture to adjoin the *Call*'s existing building and to harmonize with the existing urban fabric, the building also used, instead of a steel structure, reinforced concrete in an ingenious system of closely spaced columns to funnel loads to the ground. Wright had three models of the building made, and it became one of his favorite projects.[8]

Finding new solutions to the expanding needs of American business continued to preoccupy Wright into the 1920s. His design of the National Life Insurance Company in Chicago in 1924 was a stunning *tour de force*, expressing the functions of the building through the articulation of its massing; it also provided the opportunity to move the concept of the cantilever, which Wright saw as a revolutionary modern development, from domestic to commercial scale, so that all the floors of the building became overhangs from a central structural core of reinforced concrete (Fig. 1.6). Wright also jettisoned masonry cladding in favor of a curtain wall of glass and copper. Despite these innovations, the interior spatial layout of offices was rectilinear and conventional.

Though skyscrapers solved the needs of business, they sometimes adversely affected the urban environment by blocking light to lower buildings and the ground and by creating congestion with people and vehicles. Following up on earlier efforts in New York to control size, placement, and shape, Wright proffered his own version of zoning in a series of drawings dating to 1926 called "Skyscraper Regulation"(Fig. 1.7).[9] The drawings show how two city blocks could have flat-roofed skyscrapers limited to the edges of the blocks with the tallest buildings along the widest avenues. Multi-laned traffic would occur between blocks while open parks and access to parking are located in their centers.

The combination of Wright's effort to design a skyscraper and his interest in the varieties of forms produced through rotational geometry merged in 1929 when he designed residential towers for the Church of St. Marks-in-the-Bouwerie, intended for a location between 2nd Avenue, 10th Street, and Stuyvesant Street on an irregular lot in New York City. The Rev. William Norman Guthrie, one of Wright's early clients in the 1900s and a long-time friend and supporter, originally commissioned Wright for one tower.[10] Wright provided four towers (Figs. 1.8, 1.9; also see Catalogue Nos. 8, 10), hoping they would generate rental income for the church.

6 See Robert Sweeny, **Wright in Hollywood: Visions of a New Architecture** (New York: Architectural History Foundation; and Cambridge, Mass.: MIT Press, 1994).

7 For an overview of Wright's work in the 1920s, see David G. De Long, ed., **Frank Lloyd Wright: Designs for an American Landscape, 1922-1923** (New York: Abrams, 1996).

8 See Anthony Alofsin, "The *Call* Building: Frank Lloyd Wright's Skyscraper for San Francisco" in **Das Bauwerk und die Stadt: The Building and the Town, Essays for Eduard F. Sekler** (Vienna: Böhlau Verlag, 1994), 17-27. The *Call* building incorporated the kinds of primary forms Wright had seen in Europe, particularly multiple-framed coffering and sculptural figures rendered exclusively in prismoidal geometry.

9 See Bruce Brooks Pfeiffer, **Treasures of Taliesin: Seventy-Six Unbuilt Designs** (Fresno: The Press at California State University; and Edwardsville: and Southern Illinois University Press, 1985), plates 15a, 15b, n.p.

10 For the early connections between Guthrie and Wright, see Alofsin, **The Lost Years**, 44-46, 126, 229-231, 295, 355 n.98. I am currently working on a comprehensive, long-term study of the important relationship between Guthrie and Wright.

Figure 1.10 (Catalogue No. 11). St. Marks-in-the-Bouwerie, New York City 1929 (project). Interior view of the apartments. FLWF 2905.039. © Frank Lloyd Wright Foundation.

Figure 1.11 (Catalogue No. 13). Grouped Towers, Chicago, 1930 (project). Apartment towers. FLWF 3001.001. © Frank Lloyd Wright Foundation.

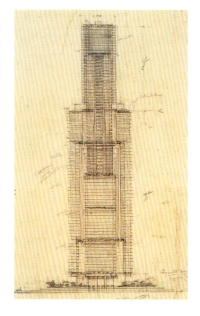

Figure 1.12 (Catalogue No. 14). Century of Progress, 1931 (project). View of skyscraper designed for Chicago World's Fair. FLWF 3103.002. © Frank Lloyd Wright Foundation.

Wright saw the trapezoidal site as an ideal opportunity for his rotational system to produce façades that shifted in response to lot lines as well as to climate and sun. After studying alternatives, Wright defined a clear concept: a deep pointed foundation would anchor the building to create a spine from which floors would be suspended, making a vertical cantilever with the mass in the ground resisting lateral forces.[11] Reinforcing the metaphor of his architecture as natural and organic, he called the core a "tap root," implying the building was a living organism fed by the soil. Three formal elements made up the plan configuration: a pinwheel rotated sixty degrees from horizontal, a square superimposed over and aligned with the pinwheel but divided into quadrants with shifts to provide offsets, and a second square superimposed over the pinwheel but oriented horizontally. A hint of the design process involved was contained in the floor slabs which were to be scored with two diamond-shaped grids, one set rotated against the other. The grid lines provided a system for locating much of the furniture and configurations of subsidiary spaces, including bathrooms and kitchens. The pinwheel's fins thickened towards the center where Wright located two ducts, vital for support services, and two elevators. The very center of the pinwheel provided no structure but allowed space for much needed trunk and storage rooms. Concrete floor slabs cantilevered from the pinwheel fins. Exterior walls consisted of screens of glass and copper.

The scheme at St. Marks-in-the-Bouwerie called for four duplex apartments per floor with each apartment having an internal stair from the lower level with its partially double-height living room to an upper-level bedroom balcony which overlooked both the living room and the exterior urban view. The interiors would have furnishings and utilities integral with the building, but they were not fully developed (Fig. 1.10). The façades also were unresolved and showed a combination of three surface motifs: a diamond over portions of the glazing; a polygon, resembling a diamond with clipped tops and bottoms providing a grill-like framing acting as a cornice at the top floor; and a combination of dynamic diagonals and rectilinear layered planes for the fascia at the floor slabs to express the floor separations on the exterior. Wright also tested a pattern using trapezoids arranged on a diagonal grid. As he did frequently in his smaller scaled ornament, he contrasted the visual diagonality of the pattern moving in one direction with a countervailing force in the opposite direction, and he articulated both sets of trapezoids with an in-fill of solid triangles in the corners of the patterns.

11 FLWF 2905.111 shows the first evidence of the "tap root."

12 See Hilary Ballon's essay "From New York to Bartlesville: The Pilgrimage of Wright's Skyscraper." in this volume, pp. 100-111.

Figure 1.13 (Catalogue No. 15). Crystal Heights, Washington, DC, 1940 (project). Elevation. FLWF 4016.003. © Frank Lloyd Wright Foundation.

Figure 1.14 (Catalogue No. 19). Rogers Lacy Hotel, Dallas Texas, 1946 (project). Exterior perspective. FLWF 4606.001. © Frank Lloyd Wright Foundation.

Wright put much effort into the St. Marks design and publicized it, but his sponsor, the Rev. Guthrie, remained uneasy about its unusual structure and appearance (see Fig. 4.3, p. 103).[12] He also increasingly doubted that the innovative design would attract tenants and guarantee the needed rental revenues to support this church, and in 1930 he withdrew his support of the project.

Despite the failure to build St. Marks, Wright saw that the plan configuration with its ability to turn in response to site, views or climatic conditions had great potential. Identifying the most innovative feature of the project as its central core projecting from deep in the earth to provide the support for cantilevered floors, he also saw that the tower concept had flexibility: towers could even by joined together and grouped as seen in a 1930 project for five linked towers on Lake Shore Drive in Chicago (Fig.1.11). In this scheme Wright even enlarged the towers, supplying six apartments per floor and a building height of 258 feet in twenty-four stories.

Wright's subsequent efforts to get a skyscraper built oscillated between the National Life type, the St. Marks type with variations, and more unique soaring spires, mostly using triangulated bases. Although the organizers of the Century of Progress Fair in Chicago rejected Wright's participation, in 1931 he proffered the design for a glass and steel skyscraper for the event (Fig. 1.12). The 112-story tower was a polemical statement that would incorporate several elements needed at the fair: parking for 12,000 cars, auditorium, gardens, and restaurant in a building that would soar to 2,000 feet in height, exceeding both the Eiffel Tower (985 feet) and Empire State Building (1,250 feet). For Crystal Heights, a speculative development in Washington, DC, Wright returned to the grouped tower configuration in 1940 (Fig. 1.13; see also Catalogue nos. 16, 17).[13] A mixed use conglomeration of residences, retail, parking, and cinema, it was a precursor of development models of the future. For his addition of a research facility to the Johnson Wax Administration building, Racine, Wisconsin, Wright used the tap root concept, but followed the vocabulary he had already established at the nearby administration building, utilizing brick, rounded corners, and tubular glass (see Fig. 2.8, p. 52). For his project for the Rogers Lacy Hotel, Dallas, Texas (1946–47), Wright used the tap root idea but added a huge atrium, thereby creating a new prototype for hotel design (Fig. 1.14). He intended the hotel to cover a city block with a mix of bars, restaurants, shops, and theater and to have a forty-seven story, 350-foot tower with façade of glass scales and floors cantilevered from a central core. The project stopped when Lacy, its wealthy client, died in 1947.

Figure 1.15 (Catalogue No. 21). Price Tower, Bartlesville, Oklahoma, 1952-1956 Perspective drawing, view from the west. FLWF 5215.001. © Frank Lloyd Wright Foundation.

Figure 1.16 Price Tower, view of tower floor construction showing multi-directional steel mesh reinforcing set over wood formwork prior to pouring concrete of floor. Photograph by Joe Price (PTAC Archives).

The Price Tower as Culmination

The opportunity to fulfill the potential of his skyscraper using rotated forms finally came with the patronage of Harold C. Price and family (Fig. 1.15). At first glance the Price Tower appears nearly identical to the prototype of St. Marks-in-the-Bouwerie, but Wright made several changes. The Church's tower was for apartments, and the plan was a pinwheel with four square, rectilinear quadrants aligned with the crosses of the pin wheel axis. The Price Tower, however, would have three offices and one duplex apartment on a typical floor. He kept the quadrant form for every apartment but superimposed a square, nestled into the pinwheel, to provide the offices. Wright transposed the core on typical floors from holding storage rooms to an open elevator lobby, and he elongated and angled the base of the Price Tower. He developed the façade design with systems of louvers, defined panel patterns in copper, and elaborated furniture, furnishings, even ashtrays, and waste baskets, all of which were composed of primary forms.

Construction began in the basement with each floor consisting of a heavy web of steel reinforcing enmeshed in concrete cast into wood forms. As each floor was cast, the next section of the central center was formed and cast, followed by another floor propped up with supports while curing until the top was reached. Because the loads of the floors were transferred to the core they could be thinner at their edges and thicker at the centers, thus saving on materials. Joe Price, Harold Price's son, documented the entire construction phase in an extended series of snap shots and a movie that show not only a perceptive grasp of the key building processes but also a sensitive artistic aesthetic. The corpus of photographs, now in the Price Tower Arts Center collection, is the most comprehensive record of the early building and its initial occupancy (Fig. 1.16).

At the core of this design process governing plan and detail was Wright's system of rotational geometry that spins squares around a pinwheel. The process can be read in multiple ways. Wright described his approach as using a "1–2 triangle" in plan.[14] Using a 30–60–90 degree triangle does produce diamond-shapes or parallelograms, but basically the plan is the result of a series of rotations of squares and grids that produce diagonal effects. The steps in the design process can be systematically analyzed in diagrams (Fig.1.17, a–j). To visualize the results Wright intended, he had his apprentices construct a six and one-half foot tall model of the building (Fig.1.18). As Wright resolved the design for the site, located along Dewey Avenue in downtown Bartlesville, he placed the pinwheel's axis in line with the cardinal points of the compass and with the north-south axis parallel the main street. The Price Tower revolved around these axes.

14 Wright, **The Story of the Tower** (New York: Horizon Press, 1956), 12.

Analytical drawings of the Price Tower

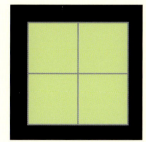 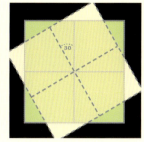 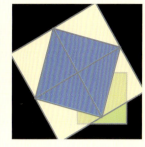 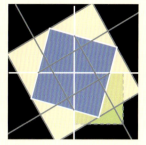

a. The scheme begins with the primary form of the square divided into four quadrants.

b. The square is copied and rotated 30°.

c. Only the bottom right quadrant of the original square is kept. An inscribed square is now inserted in the rotated square.

d. Lines are extended out from the point where the inscribed square crosses the lines that divided the orignal square into four quadrants.

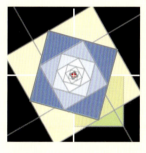 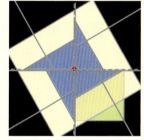 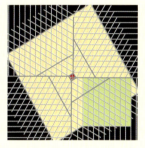 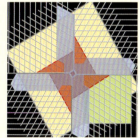

e. Additional squares are inscribed until the central medallion located on the center of every floor is formed.

f. The central space enclosed by the extended lines is marked out.

g. The grid with lines offset 2.5 ft from each other is overlaid on the plan.

h. From the grid the spaces that eventually become bathrooms and kitchens are marked out. The elevator shafts also appear.

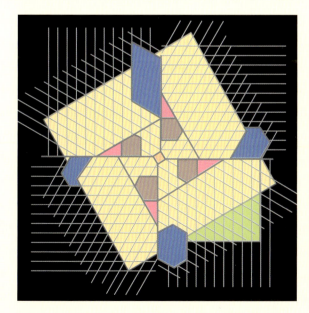 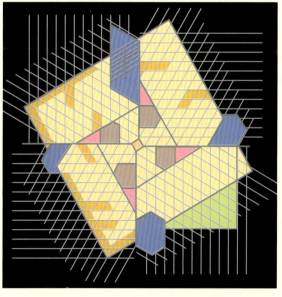

i. The green square is moved to the right and becomes the space for the dwellings. The stairwell, bathrooms and kitchen are clearly defined.

j. The last level of detail including partition walls and furniture is incorporated perfectly following the grid.

Figure 1.17 a-j   Analytical drawings of Price Tower. Credits: Edgar Bocanegra, Ricardo Ikeda, Alvaro Carrizosa, Chad Lee.

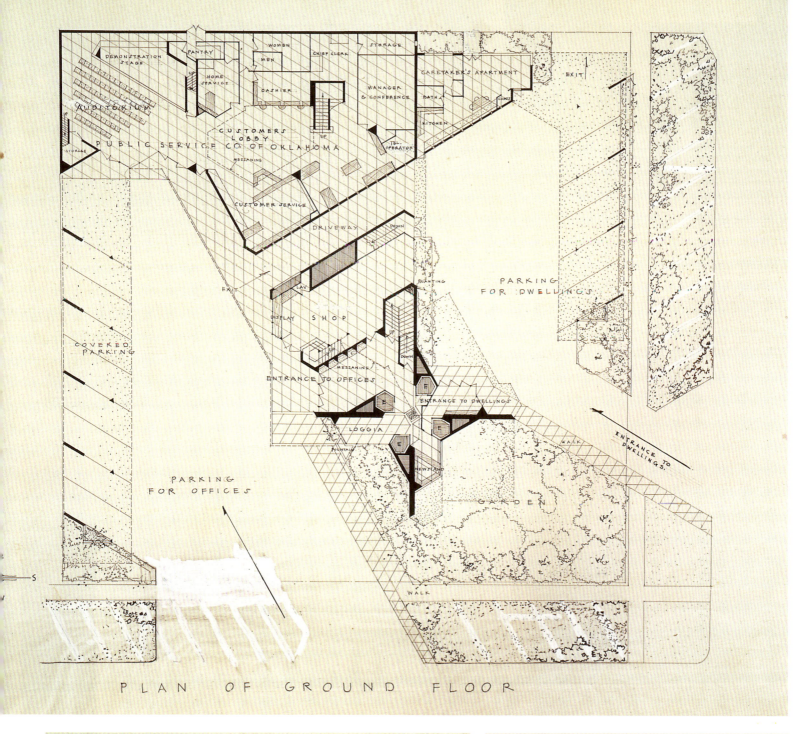

PLAN OF GROUND FLOOR

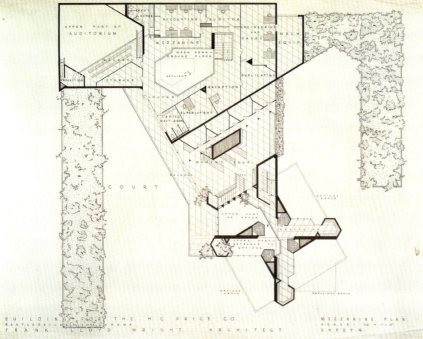

Figure 1.21 (Catalogue No. 25). Price Tower, Bartlesville, Oklahoma, 1952-1956. Ground floor plan. FLWF 5215.014. © Frank Lloyd Wright Foundation.

Figure 1.22 (Catalogue No. 26). Price Tower, Bartlesville, Oklahoma, 1952-1956. Mezzanine plan. FLWF 5215.015. © Frank Lloyd Wright Foundation.

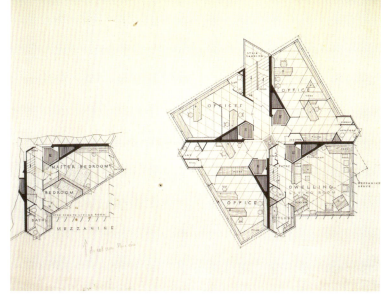

Figure 1.23 Price Tower, view into office, showing striped Philippine mahogany desks with brass edging, with matching wainscoting and built-in shelving, and glass partitions aligned with modular unit. Air diffusers are at outer edge of hung ceiling with triangular light fixtures. Windows are operable panels framed in aluminum, with exterior horizontal copper louvers. Cast aluminum office chair is at left. Photograph by Joe Price (PTAC 2003.16.284).

Figure 1.24 (Catalogue No. 27). Price Tower, Bartlesville, Oklahoma, 1952-1956. Typical tower floor plan, dwelling mezzanine. FLWF 5215.016. © Frank Lloyd Wright Foundation.

sense of dynamic movement (Fig. 1.22). The roof above the shop and office extension was intended to be a garden featuring the triangular skylight over the office atrium; office users on the east side of the tower would thus have a green garden to admire.

Starting at the third floor, Wright typically located three offices and one duplex apartment. Because of the shifted orientation of the square, the offices on each floor varied in size. Typical office layouts included desks anchored to the walls and appearing as built-in extensions of the building's angular vocabulary (Fig.1.23). Light-weight partitions, often of clear glass, separated one desk area from another, producing a small version of an open office layout. On a typical floor, elevators gave private access to either the living space level or the bedroom mezzanine above (Fig. 1.24). On the living room level, the angles of the residual spaces contained a lavatory and kitchen with custom-designed angular dining table, desks, and chairs, as well as square armchairs, which were carefully disposed about the floor (Fig. 1.25). Some views in the apartments focused inward toward a copper-sheathed fireplace; others from both the main floor and the mezzanine focused out towards the town and over the softly rolling prairie beyond. For the facing of the slab supporting the mezzanine Wright literally continued the copper cladding from the exterior across the interior space, knitting together not only interior and exterior but also the perimeters of all the mezzanines (Fig. 1.26).

The use of the typical floors changed above the fifteenth level. At the sixteenth level Wright included a commissary area for use by the Price Company. Taking advantage of the latest technology, he also included a television antenna, shaped as a spire, which projected upward. The executive apartment, intended for the Prices' occasional use and for guests, was located on the seventeenth floor, and the upper level of the apartment, as well as a small conference area, was located on the eighteenth.

H.C. Price's corporate office occupied the entire top nineteenth floor (Fig. 1.27). An elevator opened onto its tight but carefully composed reception area with built-in desk and built-in files. On its east side was an exterior stair angled into an extension of the basic pinwheel form. Entered through a door next to the elevator, Price's elegant office focused on the monogrammed floor plate as the centroid of the building. The office provided not only views from the interior, but also three openings to the exterior: from a balcony oriented southeast, a terrace with high walls on the roof of the apartment quadrant, and another terrace on the north. Wright gave special attention to the furnishings of Price's office with angular geometry governing the design of the desk, cast aluminum chairs, special copper fireplace hood, and murals (Fig.1.28).

The exterior of the Price Tower became complexly articulated as the façades have differing treatments depending on their functions as apartments or offices. While Wright's façade drawings appear flat, the experience of the building in three dimensions is dynamic: seeing the building from differing angles makes its façades appear at times open, at times closed. Gold-tinted glass behind the louvers, used to reflect the sun, adds to the visual drama. Precursors to sophisticated, contemporary thermal-controlling glazing materials, the glass appear either as golden slivers or as voids, depending on the sun's angle and viewer's perspective. The overall effect is highly kinesthetic for an object so fixed in space. By noting that vertical louvers identify the apartment quadrant and horizontal louvers identify the offices, a visitor can generally read the internal activities of the building. The top three floors with the corporate apartment and executive office are more complex, and above them the pinwheel emerges with its fins extended (Fig. 1.29). A large part of the dynamism of the exterior façades comes from the interplay of the flat surfaces, the two louver systems, and the exterior copper fascia cladding. Wright used the same basic compositional methods to achieve dynamic diagonal effects as seen in the earlier patterns at Midway Gardens, the Imperial Hotel, and his Textile Block designs.[17] At the Price Tower the copper forms were first pressed into shape from master dies (Fig. 1.30), then placed in forms before the concrete slabs were poured (Fig. 1.31). After construction, workers removed the forms and patinated the fresh copper with an acid wash to create the green effect that would normally appear over time (Fig. 1.32).

Price Tower as Precedent

With Price Tower becoming a reality, Wright lost little time in pushing forward other designs that would utilize the vocabulary and methods he had perfected in Oklahoma in the hope of establishing built versions of a new typology for the skyscraper and residential tower. His second project for Point View Residences in Pittsburgh in 1952 for Edgar Kaufmann, Sr., his client at Fallingwater, drew on the experience at Price Tower as it became a triangular apartment building with one three-thousand foot apartment per floor (Fig. 1.33).[18] Intended for senior citizens, the site proved too remote from shopping and support facilities, and Kaufmann abandoned the project. Wright's project for the Golden Beacon Apartment Tower in Chicago (1956) would have been a taller version of the Price Tower with 50 stories and a height of 482 feet (Fig. 1.34). Intended to be built upon a garage, it used vertical and horizontal fins, as at the Tower, to distinguish studios from duplex apartments. Television studios and a tower were located at the roof. Wright's former client, Charles Glore, commissioned the building for a prestigious site with great views at Lake Shore Drive and North Avenue, but despite its allure, it remained unbuilt.

Finally, Wright's Mile-High Skyscraper, his most dramatic high rise (also called "The Illinois"), would use the taproot and cantilever concepts on a tripodal base for its 528 stories. The building far exceeded the means of construction available at the time and represented a polemical challenge to contemporary skyscraper design as banal and timid. Wright compared the height of his ultimate skyscraper to an obelisk, the Pyramid of Cheops, Eiffel Tower and Empire State Building

17 See Alofsin, **The Lost Years**, 295-299.

18 Pfeiffer, **Treasures of Taliesin**, Pls. 55a, 55b with text n.p.

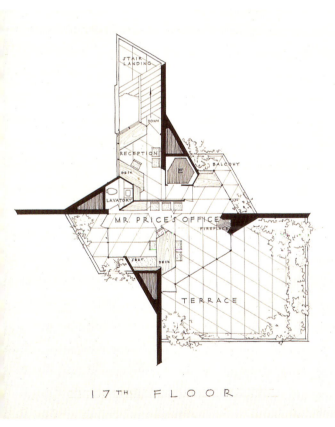

17TH FLOOR

Figure 1.29 Price Tower, detail of top floors. Photograph by Steven Brooke Studios, 2004.

Figure 1.30   Price Tower, wood formwork (shown upside down) crafted with relief pattern of ornamental copper panels, to be set inside this wood formwork before concrete is poured. Photograph by Joe Price (PTAC 2003.16.122).

Figure 1.31   Price Tower, workers setting copper panels inside wood formwork. Concrete to be poured against this inner face of copper, whose outer face is set against patterned formwork. Photograph by Joe Price (PTAC 2003.16.157).

Figure 1.32   (Catalogue Nos. 58, 59). Unpatinated and patinated copper panels. Photograph by Steven Brooke Studios, 2004.

(Fig.1.35). Displayed in dramatic renderings in Chicago in 1956, it would incorporate atomic-powered elevators and provide huge heliports, creating a "sky city." With several of these towers built, population would be concentrated to allow large expanses of open space between them.

The tall building liberated from urban congestion would continue to be a constituent element in Wright's vision of Broadacre City, his long-term project for the ideal configuration of American life in harmony with nature. Wright's images of living in the country, away from the dysfunctional city, appeared in numerous publications, including *The Living City* where the ultimate manifestation of the organic life featured the Price Tower building type (Fig. 1.36).[19]

By the time Wright died in 1959 he had seen one element of that vision embodied in a small town in Oklahoma. Harold C. Price, Wright's last great patron, died three years later. After Price's death, his family directed the business until it dissolved in 1981 and sold the Tower to the Phillips Petroleum Company. In the interim, only three apartments were used as residences. Bruce Goff lived there and had a studio from 1956 to 1963 on the ninth and tenth floors. Joe Price maintained an apartment during the time he worked for the company, and Erna and Peter Wolcott lived in an apartment from which they operated a radio station. Though five apartments were rented, many of the apartments were converted to other uses by 1972 with plans from William Wesley Peters, Wright's former son-in-law and successor at Taliesin Associated Architects. The Phillips Petroleum Company purchased the building in 1981, refurbished it in 2000, and donated it to Price Tower Arts Center the following year. The building was remodeled into eight floors of hotel rooms in 2002–2003.[20]

Wright and Price had produced a landmark in the country, a dream of a tower that would populate Wright's vision of Broadacre City, and a unique corporate headquarters, but despite the fact that Wright saw the Price Tower and the tap root design in general as a prototype for the American skyscraper, it had little connection to how the building type developed. In the first place, did the building actually have a "tap root"? Instead of the earth anchoring the building in place, the fins of its pinwheel projected straight down to a flat foundation consisting of a massive steel-laden platform which carried the weight of the building but also offset lateral loads. A literal expression of the tap root would have obstructed the central space of the basement level where the crucial heating and utility systems were located as well as the elevator lobbies on every floor. Although the analogy to a tree makes a good metaphor, where a tree is solid at its core, the Price Tower is open.

In more practical terms, the apartments were too small for families, and the offices limited in use by size. The tiny elevators were cramped and made moving

19 FLWF 5825.004, published in Wright's **The Living City** (New York: Horizon Press, 1958) also shows the Price Tower at its center.

20 For architect Wendy Evans Joseph's remodeling of the Price Tower, see the Chronology, p. 18.

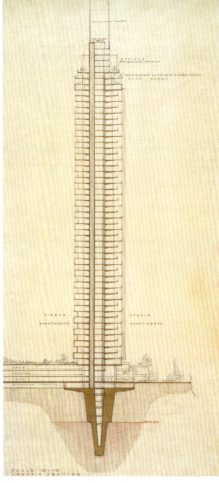

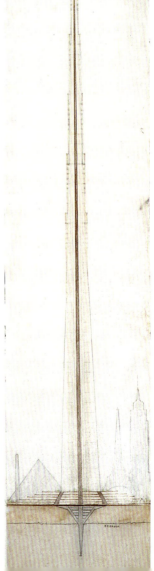

Figure 1.33 (Catalogue No. 35). Point View Residences for the Edgar J. Kaufman Charitable Trust, 1953 (project). Northwest view of apartment tower. FLWF 5310.001. © Frank Lloyd Wright Foundation.

Figure 1.34 (Catalogue No. 36). The Golden Beacon, Chicago, Illinois, 1956 (project). Cross section of apartment tower. FLWF 5615.003. © Frank Lloyd Wright Foundation.

Figure 1.35 Mile-High Skyscraper ("The Illinois"), 1956 (project). Section. FLWF 5617.00. © Frank Lloyd Wright Foundation.

Figure 1.36 (Catalogue No. 39). *The Living City*, 1958 (project). drawing for *The Living City* (New York: Horizon Press, 1958). Air view. FLWF 5825.002. © Frank Lloyd Wright Foundation.

of furniture or large objects difficult. Also, compared to other skyscrapers, the Price Tower with only nineteen floors was diminutive: the Woolworth Building (1912) had fifty floors, the Chrysler Building (1930) has over seventy-three floors, the Empire State Building (1930) has eighty-five floors, and the contemporary Seagram Building (1957), which did become an all-pervasive prototype, has thirty-eight. It was also too expensive to serve as a prototype. Costing $2.2 million dollars for its 57,315 gross square feet in 1956, it was reported to be the most expensive building in American history in terms of square foot costs.[21] Totally handcrafted, a one-off object of luxury and indulgence, the building was an aesthetic statement but lacked the financial potential that would come from using prefabricated building elements or the economics of scale which made other skyscrapers such excellent investments for American capitalism. When the costs were published, they made Price appear so rich that even a chicken farmer in India wrote requesting a loan from the man whom he saw as America's super rich titan. Price was proud of the building regardless of the cost overruns and ultimately enjoyed working with Wright.

Despite the limitations of expense and size, though, the Price Tower has many features that other skyscrapers lack. While many skyscrapers prove an economic success, few match the aesthetic impact of the small, delicate faceted jewel that is the Price Tower. It was also the rare example of skyscraper as *Gesamtkunstwerk*, harmonizing exterior and interior surfaces with details including furniture, textiles, and even chinaware. It mixed offices, apartments, retail, and public enterprise in innovative combinations. It responded to the environment and its climate, altering its elevations to sun, view, and weather.

Instead of being the end of a dream, the Price Tower might be a model for the future. The potentials of rapid prototyping might allow efficiencies unavailable to Wright, and new technology, along with revolutionary materials, might produce a new generation of custom-designed small-scale boutique skyscrapers for which the Price Tower could serve as precedent. From the perspective of business practices, dazzling digital communications and internet connections allow unprecedented global decentralization. A whole new generation of tall buildings using fresh vocabularies of twisting spirals with facades shifted to views and climate, new structural solutions, and innovative materials may find inspiration from the Price Tower, producing not merely extruded internet cafés but places for personal, human contact that counteract the isolationism of digital technology. In the future, people may need these new kinds of gathering places to congregate in smaller numbers and in smaller buildings. For all these ventures, the Price Tower, a pinwheel on the prairie, remains a fine inspiration. ■ ■ ■

21 Harold C. Price, Sr., to Frank Lloyd Wright, 30 August 1956, PTAC Archives. Revenues for 42,000 net rental space were $52 per square foot and $35.55 per square foot for the remainder. Some discrepancy exists for the final costs. (See Joseph Siry's essay in this volume for further details). At $2.2 million in 1956, the amount adjusted for inflation would be $15.42 million in 2005 at a cost of approximately $269 per square foot. (Bureau of Labor Statistics).

WRIGHT'S PRICE TOWER: CONTEXT, CLIENTS, AND CONSTRUCTION

Joseph M. Siry

Frank Lloyd Wright's Price Tower marked the culmination of forty years of his ideas about rethinking the structural and visual form of the tall building. This late tower is clearly situated in his *oeuvre* as the realization of a new kind of skyscraper with deep roots in Wright's earlier built and unbuilt projects. Yet the Price Tower was equally meaningful in its context of Bartlesville, Oklahoma, where it stood in dialogue with earlier tall buildings of different patronage, structure, and form (Figs. 2.1a, 2.1b). Wright's prairie skyscraper was the project of the Price family as a collective client involved in every phase of the design's development, realization, and presentation to its local and distant audiences. The Price Tower thus stands at the intersection of multiple histories. Its place in Wright's own thinking about the architectural art is a central question, but his ideas for this building also connect to issues of context and client, and to works of his predecessors and contemporaries in the engineering and aesthetics of the modern skyscraper.

Bartlesville, the Oil Industry, and the Tall Building as Corporate Monument

To study Bartlesville's history and architecture is to appreciate the financial power of the oil and gas industries to shape a community in its landscape. For Wright the Price Tower was to be a perfected architectural object previously conceived for his imagined utopia of Broadacre City. Yet from the perspective of its clients, the building was an outgrowth of their immersion in the life of their business centered in Bartlesville, where Oklahoma's oil and gas industry began when oil was first commercially extracted from local wells in 1897. From that time, the town's growth focused initially on the leases for drilling rights at surrounding properties controlled by H. Vernon Foster (1875-1939), who owned a general drilling lease over a large acreage belonging to the Osage Nation. Regional reserves were so great that by 1904, seven years after the town's first paying well was dug, there were one hundred and fifty oil companies with offices in Bartlesville. Foster grew to be the region's richest man both by drilling successful wells himself and by subleasing rights to pioneering companies, including those of George and J. Paul Getty, and Frank and Lee E. Phillips. Foster's fortune enabled him to build a large country house on a fifty-two-acre estate southeast of town called La Quinta in 1932.[1]

Before the Prices acquired their own estate nearby and built their home on it in 1947, the family had leased the former Foster house at 821 Johnstone Avenue from 1933, after Foster moved to La Quinta. Harold C. Price, Sr. (1888-1962), had achieved unique success as a founding partner in a company launched in 1921 to provide welding services to the region's oil producers. Their vast tank farms for oil storage stretched both east and west of Bartlesville. Graduated from the Colorado School of Mines in 1912, Price had come to Bartlesville to work as a chemist for a local zinc smelting company before serving in the Army during the First World War. After the zinc company failed in 1921, Price, with support from his brother Joseph M. Price in New York and his partner J. F. Lincoln, began their company to pioneer electric rather than acetylene welding. This innovation proved superior in terms of its rapidity, safety, and reliability, and, after his partner left to start another company, Price expanded his firm into a builder of oil and gas pipelines in the southwestern United States, Venezuela, and Alaska, through the Second World War. H.C. Price Co. was its industry's leader in technical innovations for the coating and laying of pipelines. These included the Big Inch that runs 1,341 miles from Longview, Texas, to New Jersey, built by the federal government in 1942-43 to provide a safe overland method of transporting crude oil during World War II. By the time the Price Tower's construction began, the company had built over 21,000 miles of pipelines in projects through North and South America and the Middle East. The Price Company's

FOOTNOTES

This essay is part of a broader study, still in preparation, of the Price Tower and its construction. Research for this essay was done during the priod of an N.E.H. Summer Stipend (FT-52659-04). Any views, findings, conclusions, or recommendations expressed in this publication do not necessarily reflect those of the National Endowment for the Humanities.

1 On Foster, see William Donohue Ellis, **Out of the Osage: The Foster Story** (Oklahoma City: Oklahoma Heritage Association, 1993; rev. ed., 1994). La Quinta was designed in the Spanish Mission style by Edward Buehler Delk (1885-1956), an architect based in Kansas City who did extensive work in Tulsa and Bartlesville, and who later worked as a local associate of Frank Lloyd Wright on projects in Kansas City. See "La Quinta: A Country Home in Bartlesville, Oklahoma, Follows the Spanish Mission Style," **Country Life** 69 (November 1935): 20-25. On Delk, see **Selections from the Work of Edward Buehler Delk, Architect, Kansas City, Missouri** (New York: Architectural Catalog Company, 1935); and Thomas E. Young, **Edward Buehler Delk, Architect** (Tulsa: Philbrook Museum of Art, 1993). On the building's history, see Joanne Riney Bennett and Patricia Dewar Cordell, **A Pictorial History of Bartlesville** (Bartlesville: Washington County Historical Society, 1972).

Figure 2.1a   Price Tower, northeast corner, Dewey Avenue and Sixth Street, Bartlesville, Okla., looking southeast. View taken from the Phillips Tower (1962-63). Courtesy of the Bartlesville Area History Museum.

pipeline construction business was valued at $10 million. H.C. Price Co. was privately held. No stock was publicly traded. Members of the Price family owned most of the company's stock, yet Harold Price encouraged profit sharing through employee stock purchases which he underwrote. This helped to shape an extraordinarily loyal and committed work force over the years. Price never reported to stockholders or directors. This left him free to make all decisions, including hiring Wright for the Price Tower.[2]

The success of these projects enabled the Price family to relocate and commission its first work of architecture. In 1926 Harold Price had married Mary Lou Patteson (1900-1978), a graduate of the University of Oklahoma and a schoolteacher in Bartlesville. Like their sons, Harold C. Price, Jr. (1927-) and Joseph D. Price (1929-), Mrs. Price was immersed in the company, and together the family of four would serve as "the building committee" with Frank Lloyd Wright.[3] In the early 1940s, the Prices had purchased an estate of over one hundred acres, the Star View Farm, southeast of Bartlesville just beyond La Quinta, where they planned to raise horses. In searching for an architect, Mrs. Price was drawn to the ranch houses of Cliff May (1908-1989) in southern California, as featured in *Sunset* magazine.[4] The Prices also knew of May's work from their vacations in Los Angeles, La Jolla, and Santa Barbara from 1931, and Harold Price, Sr., made contact with May while working in southern California. The long, low one-story ranch house that May designed for the Prices featured shingled roofs overhanging walls of thin-coursed fieldstone. Outdoor flagstone patios extended into surrounding gardens, accented by a broad chimney and dovecote-like tower, all characteristic of May's style (Fig. 2.2). Interiors featured wood paneling and many hand-wrought details in the spirit of the Arts and Crafts movement. The Price house was May's first in Oklahoma, and Harold Price, Jr., remembers it as the "first really different house built in Bartlesville.... Everything else was just very much like everything that was being built at that time. Cliff May was different."[5] The Prices were very pleased with the house and with May. Later, when Wright was in Bartlesville in connection with the tower, and had proposed to design a new house for Harold Price, Jr., he also visited the Cliff May house. Expecting that Wright would propose to build his parents a new house as well, Price recalls that instead Wright said to his parents, "Ah, you don't need a house by me. This is fine." Only later would Wright design an exceptional house for the elder Prices in Arizona.[6]

In 1952 the Prices began to contemplate a new office building for their company, which, before it was housed in Wright's tower, rented offices in the Union National Bank building. The company's expansion demanded additional administrative space, but the Prices were also responding in part to Bartlesville's earlier commercial architecture. The most prominent corporate monuments were those of Phillips Petroleum Co., incorporated by Frank Phillips (1873-1950) and his brothers in 1917. By the company's tenth anniversary in 1927, its plants produced one eighth of all the natural gasoline manufactured in the United States, and the company entered the retail marketing of automobile fuel. The monument to this early phase of corporate growth was the Frank Phillips Building, begun in 1925 as a seven-story block on the northeast corner of Fourth and Johnstone streets. Soon they added to their new quarters an eighth floor and corner tower in an Italian Renaissance style (Fig. 2.3).[7]

The Frank Phillips Building was an architectural sign of Bartlesville's dependence on outside capital investment in the era when Phillips and others took oil to Wall

2   Bill Creel, former employee of H. C. Price Co., interview with Sue Lacey and Arn Henderson, 21 August 1990, 20. PTAC Archives. The company's value was noted in "Skyscraper Cast Its Shadow on the Plains," **Business Week**, 18 February 1956, 114. On the company's miles of pipelines, see "October to See Start of Price Tower," **Tulsa Tribune**, 1 October 1953. On the company's history from its founding in 1921, see Frederick L. Rice, **The Silver Tie-In: Twenty-Five Years of Pioneering in Electric Welding** (Bartlesville, Okla.: H.C. Price Co., 1946), and in **Fifty Years; H.C. Price Co. 1921/1971**. The company's own semi-annual newsletter, **The Tie-In**, traced its activities as did its industry's periodicals like **Pipe Line Industry** (Houston), **The Pipeliner**, **The Oil and Gas Journal**, **Gas Magazine**, and **Gas**. The Price family's occupancy of the former Foster home in town was noted in Joe Price, interview with George M. Goodwin, 10 April 1993. Price Tower Arts Center (subsequently referred to as PTAC) Archives.

3   On Price family history, see "H.C. Price Dies, Services Tuesday," **Bartlesville Examiner-Enterprise**, 29 January 1962, and on Mrs. Price, see "H.C. Price Co-Founder Dies Monday," **Bartlesville Examiner-Enterprise**, 24 January 1978. See also HCPJr, interview with George Goodwin, 10 April 1993. PTAC Archives. The senior Harold's elder brother, Joseph M. Price (d.1949), was a wealthy dress manufacturer in New York City, where he championed urban political reform through the Fusion movement that had opposed Tammany Hall. The elder Joseph Price and his wife Miriam Sutro Price (d.1957) long supported Robert Moses, who was a friend of the Price family, as were the Roosevelts. See Joseph M. Price, "Fusion Mistakes and a Way Out," **National Municipal Review** 7 (March 1918): 183-6; Robert A. Caro, **The Power Broker: Robert Moses and the Fall of New York** (New York: Alfred A. Knopf, 1974), 200, 348, 350, 352, 356, 435, 436-7, 438, 567; and Gerard H. Davis, "The Success of Fusion Reform in 1933," Ph.D. diss., Columbia U., 1977. HCPJr recalled that his uncle Joe and aunt Miriam had a big influence on the Oklahoma family. They were interested in the arts, Miriam having been a roommate of Gertrude Stein at Radcliffe and a friend of Gertrude's brother, Leo Stein. He and his wife were collectors of Matisse and patrons of Le Corbusier's Villa Stein-De Monzie, near Paris (1926-27). HCPJr also recalled that on one occasion, his father, Wright, Gordon Bunshaft, and Robert Moses lunched in New York, where Harold Price, Sr., encouraged Wright to tell people that his buildings were going to cost more than conventional ones, but that they were worth it. Wright, however, insisted that his architecture should not cost more.

4   On Cliff May, see **Sunset Magazine**, in collaboration with Cliff May, **Sunset Western Ranch Houses** (San Francisco: Lane, 1946); Cliff May and Paul C. Johnson, **Western Ranch Houses** (1958; repr., Santa Monica, Calif.: Hennessey and Ingalls, 1997); Charles Moore, Peter Becker, and Regula Campbell, **The City Observed: Los Angeles** (New York: Random House, 1984), 185-87; and Cliff May and Marlene L. Laskey, **The California Ranch House** (Los Angeles: Oral History Program, UCLA, 1984).

5   Harold C. Price, Jr. (subsequently referred to as HCPJr), interview with George M. Goodwin, 10 April 1993. PTAC Archives.

6   Ibid. PTAC Archives. Wesley Peters similarly recalled Wright's view of the Cliff May home, "He thought it was pretty nice space and he complimented on how the house was ordered and worked rather well for their purpose. But once he told Mr. Price I believe, 'Hal, this is a nice house but it's not up to your style' or something like that." William Wesley Peters, interview with Gregory Williams and Sue Lacey, 27 February 1990, 20. PTAC Archives.

7   The tower is the only portion of the original Frank Phillips Building that remains today. With the demolition of the adjacent block, 43,000 bricks were saved to finish the south and east sides of the Frank Phillips Tower Center, encasing the tower's lower stories on its east side. The adjacent fifteen-story Plaza Office Building (1984-86), designed by Hellmuth, Obata, and Kassabaum, is the company's largest office facility in Bartlesville, set in an entire city block amid parks and fountains. ["Bartlesville Facility Facts," ConocoPhillips Corporate Archives, Bartlesville, n.d.] The original Frank Phillips Tower is distinct from the later Phillips Building (1962-63), designed by Welton Becket of Los Angeles and built by George A. Fuller Co. of New York, sited east of Johnstone Avenue across from the Adams Building.

Figure 2.1b   Price Tower, northeast corner, Dewey Avenue and Sixth Street, Bartlesville, Okla., looking southeast. View taken from the Phillips Tower (1962-63). Courtesy of the Bartlesville Area History Museum.

Figure 2.2   Cliff May, Harold C. Price, Sr., House, Star View Farm, Bartlesville, 1946-48. PTAC Archives.

Figure 2.3   Frank Phillips Building, northeast corner, Johnstone Avenue and Fourth Street, Bartlesville, 1925-27. Courtesy of the Bartlesville Area History Museum.

Figure 2.4 Neville, Sharp, and Simon, Adams Building, Phillips Petroleum Company, Johnstone Avenue front, between Fourth and Fifth streets, Bartlesville, in construction, 1948-50, showing reinforced concrete frame, with entrance canopy to 1928 Phillips Building in foreground on Fourth Street. Courtesy of Bartlesville Area History Museum.

Figure 2.5 Adams Building, Phillips Petroleum Company, Bartlesville, as completed, 1950. Courtesy of ConocoPhillips Archives, Bartlesville.

Figure 2.6 Gentry and Voskamp, Phillips Apartment Hotel, Johnstone Avenue, between Eighth and Ninth streets, Bartlesville, ready for occupancy, 1949. Courtesy of ConocoPhillips Archives, Bartlesville, photograph 305-9-a.

Street. As the head of the company in the boom period of the 1920s, he led something of a double life as both head of operations in Oklahoma and the company's ambassador in New York City. There he succeeded in convincing bankers, brokers, investors, and directors that Phillips Petroleum was a solid investment and that the company's operations and bookkeeping were beyond doubt. He occupied quarters at the Plaza Hotel until 1921 and then at the Ambassador on Park Avenue, which opened that year. He then also leased offices at the Equitable Building at 120 Broadway between Pine and Cedar streets. In 1931 the company moved to the new Irving Trust Building at Broadway and Wall Street. In this context, the Phillips Building in Bartlesville echoed such monuments to financial power in Manhattan, the word Phillips chose as the name of his personal railroad car.[8]

In the decade after World War II, Phillips Petroleum Co.'s expansion as a supplier of natural gas, gasoline, and petrochemicals made it the fastest growing of the twenty largest oil companies. The firm's major statement in architecture just prior to the Price Tower was the twelve-story Adams Building, opened late in 1950, designed by Neville, Sharp and Simon of Kansas City and named for President Kenneth S. "Boots" Adams, who had headed the company since 1938 (Figs. 2.4, 2.5). Sited on an entire city block bounded east and west by Johnstone and Jennings avenues between Fourth and Fifth streets, south of the earlier Phillips Tower, the Adams Building consolidated over half the company's 3,300 employees, previously scattered in thirty-five different locations around Bartlesville. The perfectly rectangular block contained 415,000 square feet (9.5 acres) of office space, and was designed for additional wings if needed. Structurally, the Adams Building was a steel-reinforced concrete frame clad in brick. Its auditorium, assembly, conference and club rooms, library, medical center, cafeteria, and gymnasium made it the center of what had become an international corporation. Its interiors were surfaced with twenty-nine different types of marble from seven states and six foreign countries. A panorama of mural photographs along the lobby's balcony showed the oil industry's history. As one of the largest buildings in the southwest, the Adams Building cost $13 million, or over six times the eventual cost of the Price Tower, which was completed for $2.1 million.[9]

Rapid growth through the war had accelerated demand for housing as well as offices, and Phillips lost numerous employees who could not find adequate dwellings for their families in Bartlesville, whose population climbed to 19,228 by 1950. Thus, concurrent with the Adams Building, the company built the seven-story Phillips Apartment Hotel (now the Hotel Phillips), on the west side of Johnstone Avenue between Eighth and Ninth streets. Designed by Gentry and Voskamp of Kansas City, the building was announced in 1948 and opened June 1, 1950 (Fig. 2.6). The apartments were built on the site of the H. V. Foster House at 821 Johnstone Avenue, which the Prices had been renting and had to vacate, prompting them to commission May for their ranch house. As Bartlesville's first modern apartment building, this 206-unit structure was to meet a large demand for apartments among single employees and childless married couples, supplementing the company's investment in single-family homes in southwest Bartlesville. There were also rooms for temporary out-of-town employees or guests. Like the Adams Building, the Phillips Apartment Hotel was built by the Manhattan Construction Company of Muskogee as a reinforced concrete frame clad in brick with horizontally proportioned windows between columns. Modern details included its corner windows and flat roof, which served as a sun deck, as well as air conditioning, self-service elevators (when the town's other buildings had full-time elevator operators), and fourteen varied color schemes for apartments.[10]

8 On Phillips's residences and offices in Manhattan, see Michael Wallis, **Oil Man: The Life of Frank Phillips and Phillips Petroleum** (New York: Doubleday, 1988), 169, 171-72, 175-76, 193, 323. The original Phillips Tower in Bartlesville of 1928 was also a local extension of a regional Art Deco architectural style centered in Tulsa, where the building it most resembled was the twenty-seven story National Bank of Tulsa (1918, 1922; Weary and Alford).

9 "Bartlesville Tower Rises, Oddest Building in State," **Tulsa World**, 21 February 1955. Information on materials is found in Phillips Petroleum Co., Tour Guide Manual for the Phillips and Adams Buildings, 1965. ConocoPhillips Archives, Bartlesville.

10 The single-family houses southwest of Bartlesville were designed as the Jane Phillips Addition. On the Adams Building and Phillips Apartment Hotel, see "Phillips Will Construct Two Big Buildings," **Tulsa World**, 15 August 1948 and "Comfortable, Convenient Living," **Philnews** (January 1951): 16-17. ConocoPhillips Archives, Bartlesville.

The later Price Tower's apartments would be evaluated against this standard, as its offices would be compared to the Adams Building's. Since the 1920s Harold Price, Sr., had known Phillips socially in Bartlesville, and the Price Company had done work for Phillips Petroleum. Yet Harold Price, Jr., recalls that when his family decided to build their building, "We didn't like what Phillips had put up in Bartlesville. We just didn't think the structures were attractive, and we were all very proud of the community."[11] According to both of his sons, Harold Price, Sr., initially envisioned a one- to four-story, ranch-style office building, possibly designed by Cliff May. The Price Company would occupy about 50,000 square feet and rent out the additional office space of which there was then a local shortage. The elder Price initially envisioned the site next to the modern Bartlesville College High School southeast of town.[12] His son Joe Price had learned about Wright from architect Bruce Goff. Long an admirer of Wright's work, Goff had taught since 1947 at the University of Oklahoma's School of Architecture, when the Price sons were both studying at the university. Under Goff's chairmanship of the school, Wright had lectured there and had praised its educational program.[13] Inspired by Goff, Joe Price had asked him if he would be interested in designing the Price building, but Goff, although he said he would like to do it, advised that if the Prices "really wanted the best architect, to get Frank Lloyd Wright."[14] Joe Price recalled meeting Wright at one of his university lectures, and encouraged his father to contact Wright, of whom the family had heard.

While the Prices had not read Wright's *Autobiography* (first published in 1932 and in an expanded edition of 1943), they had read Ayn Rand's *The Fountainhead* (1943), whose fictional architect-hero Howard Roark is thought to have been modeled at least partially on Wright. Harold Price, Jr., recalled that the family had not seen Wright's buildings in Chicago, Los Angeles, or elsewhere, even though they had regularly visited southern California. As a young man, Harold Price, Sr., had painted recreationally, and the family had visited the Metropolitan Museum (not the Museum of Modern Art) when in New York. They did not yet know of Goff when they had asked Cliff May to design their house, and Harold Price, Jr., recalled, that "my parents I don't think would have been comfortable in a Bruce Goff house at all. My Dad was very conservative…so was my mother. In artistic expression they were conservative." The young Harold "knew nothing about the conflicts in architecture at that time. All I knew was what I read in *The Fountainhead*. [I] liked the democratic philosophy, architectural philosophy, that was expressed in that. I knew that was Wright's approach but I didn't have a real analytical knowledge of that at all."[15]

In April 1952 Harold Price, Jr., had an initial conversation with Wright by telephone, indicating that they wanted to build a four-story building, and Wright invited the family to Taliesin. The Prices, parents and sons, and a company officer flew in their own plane to Spring Green, Wisconsin, on 10 June, where they were met by Wesley Peters and driven to Taliesin. Both sons recalled that their father knew what he wanted, and they thought that he might not get along with Wright. Upon arriving, they walked around the house and gardens, and Joe Price recalls that his father upon seeing Taliesin said that "this isn't any better than our house back in Bartlesville." However, his attitude visibly changed when he saw the cornerstone near the house's front door, which gave the house's date. The elder Price was impressed that Taliesin, which he mentally compared to May's ranch house of 1948, was more than thirty-five years older, yet Wright had designed a dwelling that was comparably modern in character if not similar in materials to May's work.[16]

11 HCPJr, interview with George M. Goodwin, 10 April 1993. PTAC Archives. In a television appearance after the tower opened, Wright said that in Bartlesville "the Phillips Oil people have built these large business buildings. To me they're of course, boxes and ugly. Now why not the same impetus? Here's the Price Pipeline Construction Company. Big Inch, Little Inch, and so on, wanted to build a building. They wanted to build another building like the Phillips people. And I said, why not do something to grace your own town? Why not take the skyscraper, make an ideal thing of it, there as beautiful as a tree, and enjoy it yourselves?" FLW, transcript of remarks on Tex and Jinx McCrary's program, WRCA-TV, New York, 23 April 1956, attached to Kenneth S. "Boots" Adams to Harold C. Price, 3 May 1956. PTAC Archives.

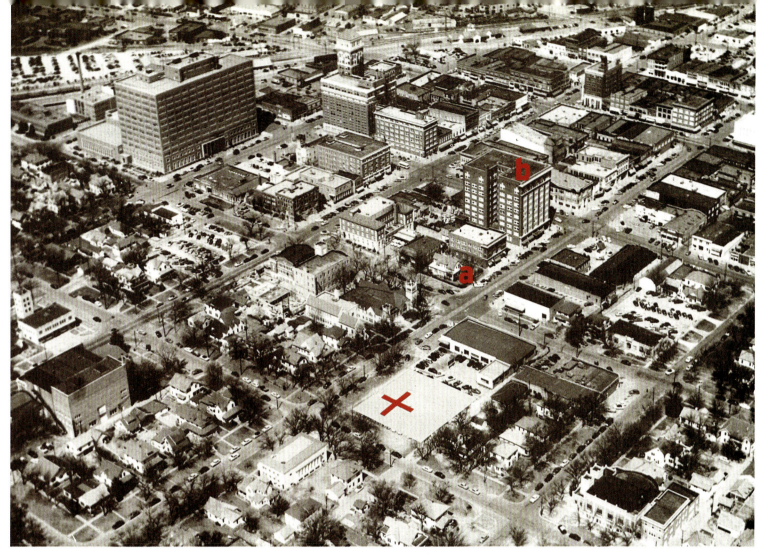

Figure 2.7 Aerial view, downtown Bartlesville, showing (a) original lot selected for Price Tower, northwest corner, Dewey Avenue and Fifth Street, (b) Cities' Service Oil Company, southwest corner, Dewey and Fourth, and (X) future site of Price Tower as built, northeast corner, Dewey and Sixth. Photograph by D.S. Willcox, from Wright, **Story of the Tower** (1956).

12 HCPJr, interview with George M. Goodwin, 10 April 1993. PTAC Archives. Joe Price recalled that if his father and Wright had not gotten along well, then the elder Price "would have had a two-story ranch-style office building designed by Cliff May." Joe Price, interview with George M. Goodwin, 10 April 1993. PTAC Archives. Joe Price recalled that his father, before approaching Wright, "had always wanted to build a ranch-style office building near College High School. He had the land picked out. It wasn't purchased but it was picked out, just to the south of College High." The site was at the corner of Hillcrest. Joe Price, interview with Sue Lacey, 26 February 1990, 1. PTAC Archives. Perhaps Wright in retrospect alluded to this possible alternative design for the Price Company office building when he wrote of their tower-to-be, "With even more privacy and no less convenience than the ranch-type pancake down in the dust, such a building confers not only added distinction to the owner and occupants but to the town." Wright, "Notes on the Structure for the Harold C. Price Company of Bartlesville, Oklahoma," Taliesin West, April 1953. FLWA/PTAC Archives. Wright, **Story of the Tower** (New York: Horizon Press, 1956), 19, had similarly written, "Steel, the spider spinning, here serves the democratic principle well—the individual's healthy aspiration—with even more privacy and greater convenience than the lower structures or the ranch house type lower down in the dust in this region."

13 On Goff and Wright at the University of Oklahoma, see David G. De Long, **Bruce Goff: Toward Absolute Architecture** (New York: The Architectural History Foundation; and Cambridge, Mass.: MIT Press, 1988), 87-88. According to Joe Price, his father didn't "give a hoot about art," whereas Joe "had seen a Wright-designed office building for San Francisco and was impressed by it. He persuaded his father to go see it and then to talk to Wright." Joanne Gordon, "The Skyscraper that Shocks Oklahoma Town," **Kansas City Star,** 11 March 1956. The only tall building that Wright designed for San Francisco was his unbuilt project of 1912 for the *Press* or San Francisco *Call* Building. Wright had lectured at the University of Oklahoma on 23 October 1946 (Henry L. Kamphoefner to Eugene Masselink, 22 April, 20 June, and 17 October 1946, FLWA, microfiche nos. Ø028B03, Ø028D10, Ø029C02) and on 2 May 1952 (Goff to FLW, 16 October 1950 and 22 April 1952, FLWA, microfiche nos. Ø037D07, G126E07; Ben Allen Park to FLW, 5 May 1952, FLWA, microfiche no. Ø040D01). HCPJr had graduated from the university in 1951. HCPJr's wife, Carolyn Price, who was at the university with Harold, Jr., and Joe around 1950, remembered that they together attended Wright lectures there. Carolyn Price, in conversation with author, 8 June 2004.

14 HCPJr, interview with George M. Goodwin, 10 April 1993. PTAC Archives.

15 Ibid. Howard Roark's extended statement of his philosophy of individual creativity in modern American architecture appears near the end of the novel. See Ayn Rand, **The Fountainhead** (1943; New York: Scribner, 1968), 710-717. The Prices' interest in the novel may have been prompted by the release of the film version in 1949. See recently Merrill Schleier, "Ayn Rand and King Vidor's Film *The Fountainhead* : Architectural Modernism, the Gendered Body, and Political Ideology," **JSAH** 61 (September 2002): 310-331.

16 Joe Price, interview with George M. Goodwin, 10 April 1993. PTAC Archives. In this and other interviews, Joe Price recalls the date on the cornerstone at Taliesin as 1903, yet the house was originally built in 1911-13, and rebuilt after fires of 1914 and 1925. Wright's nearby Hillside Home School was built 1901-02, but the Price interviews do not refer to it.

ed to spend."[23] He recalled of the family's first meeting with Wright, "At the idea of building a tower, my Dad was enthralled—he thought it was a great idea, since it wouldn't cost us any more money. We told [Wright] we wanted to spend $700,000—maybe it was $750,000—somewhere in there. We didn't want to spend an awful lot of money."[24]

Wright may have also convinced the Prices to find another site, which they did in the summer of 1952. Their original lot, on the northwest corner of Fifth Street and Dewey Avenue (Fig. 2.7, "a"), framed by low commercial blocks, was east of the four-story Civic Center and across Fifth Street from the Presbyterian Church with its corner tower. This original site was on the same block as the Cities' Service Oil Company's headquarters on the southwest corner of Dewey Avenue and Fourth Street (Fig. 2.7, "b"). On 19 August Harold Price wrote to Wright of the new lot a block further south from the town's center on the northeast corner of Dewey and Sixth Street (Fig. 2.7, "X" mark), "We consider this location better than the first one because we are surrounded only by low buildings, whereas in the other case we were surrounded by four-story buildings and one church, and in the midst of the heaviest traffic in town. This plot of land will lend itself better to landscaping."[25] The new larger plot, on which the Price Tower was built, was 150 by 140 feet, or one quarter of a city block. This would give the tower (about forty-five feet on a side) a wide platform of ground around its base. There Wright would design a spreading structure similar to the low parking structure around the base of the SC Johnson Tower (Fig. 2.8).

Once convinced that they could build a tower for no greater expense per square foot than their original idea of a three- or four-story building, the Prices set the parameters of cost that would frame the subsequent process of design and construction. The decision to build a tall building whose financial viability depended on office and apartment rentals was remarkable, given that there was no precedent for such a structure in Bartlesville and thus no wealth of local information on real estate ventures by which to gauge the project. The Prices were extraordinary clients in that they were willing to fund an isolated tower in their small prairie town, wherein rental returns were uncertain. Harold Price, Sr.'s decision was motivated not only by pride in his company's achievements, but also by his legendary civic commitment. Price consulted long with local civic and business leaders before deciding to erect his structure. As Wright said in spring 1956, after the tower was finished, "Bartlesville was the pleasantest small town in the United States and the home of one American citizen who had the good sense to stay home and do his stuff to make his own home-town [sic] beautiful instead of barging in on the big cities to boost rents."[26]

23 HCPJr, interview with George M. Goodwin, 10 April 1993. PTAC Archives. HCPSr to FLW, 16 June 1952, wrote, "First, I want to tell you how much all of us enjoyed the trip to Taliesin and to again thank you for your hospitality. Incidentally we had an extremely nice visit in the Johnson Wax Building. Mr. [John] Halama [architect for builder Ben Wiltscheck] showed us everything in the old building and in the new. It was indeed very interesting." FLWA, microfiche no. P122A04.

24 HCPJr, interview with Sue Lacey, 24 February 1990, 2. PTAC Archives.

25 HCPSr to FLW, 19 August 1952. FLWA. Price here also informed Wright, "The development of this project has been worked in conjunction with the Public Service Corporation of Oklahoma. They owned the first lot considered, and in order to obtain the present lot we bought theirs and traded it in on the lot we now own."

26 FLW to HCPSr 11 May 1956. FLWA, microfiche no. P149A01. PTAC Archives. Price wrote of his tower, "We all appreciated the benefits we had received from living in our community, a community that had been very helpful to a young man with no material assets. Therefore, we desired to build a structure which would be a credit to our city for years to come." Wright, **Story of the Tower**, 9. Price was particularly known for his charity toward local children, sponsoring Little League baseball and other events. ("Harry's Column," **Bartlesville Record**, 5 June 1953, and "H.C. Price Dies, Services Tuesday," **Bartlesville Examiner-Enterprise**, 29 January 1962). He headed the Chamber of Commerce, and was also an initiator of the Bartlesville Boys Club, for which he was instrumental in building a swimming pool on the town's west side, in collaboration with the Phillips Foundation. Price worked to create a public recreational site, Sooner Park, on land that his family donated to the city after his death in 1962. HCPJr, telephone conversation with author, 20 July 2004. It was noted that "Months of planning and consultation with various architects, engineers, civic and business leaders preceded the decision to erect the Price Tower." "Price Tower Will Be Built in Bartlesville," **Construction News Monthly** (10 June 1953): 117.

Figure 2.9 (Catalogue No. 22). Price Tower, Bartlesville, Oklahoma, 1952-1956. Perspective drawing, view from the south, 30 September 1952, showing outline of fountain atop air-conditioning block to right of tower. FLWF 5215.004. © Frank Lloyd Wright Foundation.

The Price Company would pay for the building out of its own resources, without the borrowed funds that would have increased pressures on rental return and construction speed. Yet if Price could be more flexible and patient than most speculative investors, in terms of the rate and rapidity of return, then he did plan to recover building costs with rentals. He soon wrote to Wright, "We will need three stories ourselves, and the Public Service Company [the local utilities supplier] will need two or three, including the first floor....This will leave four or more floors to be rented. The question of how much space we can rent will depend largely upon the rental charge, which will, in turn, depend upon the cost of the building. Naturally we prefer to build as tall a building as possible, of course depending upon our needs....We understand that the present cost of a fire proof [sic] structure would be somewhere between $18 and $20 per square foot, including architect's fees. I think you concurred in these figures. Using that figure, we are tentatively basing our rental at $3 per square foot per year, using the gross footage. This is a high price, compared to the rent that has been paid here in the past on old buildings. Therefore, if we intend to get occupancy of others, we must not let our construction costs go above the figures mentioned."[27] Ultimately the realized tower was far more costly than the Prices imagined, and the project proved a strain financially, but they were able to charge higher rents for office space, and they prized Wright's building that defined them to the world.

Wright's Original Design for the Price Tower, 1952
With a site secured and a budget framed, Wright began work on the design in late August 1952, after the Prices informed him that they needed final plans within four months of 15 July as a condition of their acquiring the site.[28] The preliminary program included apartments as well as offices, in order to increase the building's rental income, and its height. Harold Price wrote that, given their preference to build as tall as possible, "the idea of including living apartments in the building was suggested. There is a demand in Bartlesville for what might be called de luxe apartments. That is, two bedrooms and two baths, one large size living room with adjacent dinette and kitchen. It was our tentative thought that we might put two of these on a floor and use three floors of the building."[29] The apartments were intended for Price employees who also worked in the building.[30]

Wright and his assistants developed the preliminary plans and sketches for the Price Tower through September 1952 and in early October showed the design to the Prices on their second visit to Taliesin. A definitive rendering, dated 30 September 1952, shows the building from the south (Fig. 2.9).[31] Harold Price, Jr., recalled, "Wright took us in and showed us this beautiful design of a sixteen-story tower. My Dad just loved it and he and Wright hit it off in the beginning. We thought

27 HCPSr to FLW, 19 August 1952. FLWA.

28 Curtis Besinger, **Working with Mr. Wright, What It Was Like** (New York: Cambridge University Press, 1997), 242, recalled, "With the completion in August [1952] of the preliminary drawings for the [Raul] Bailleres house [in Acapulco, Mexico], Mr. Wright shifted his attention to the office building for the H. C. Price Company." Price wrote that a transaction with the Public Service Corporation, the utility company which had helped the Prices to acquire the site, "has been made with the understanding that we finalize our plans within four months from July 15th; therefore, we are obligated to the Public Service Corporation to proceed with some definite plans before the expiration of that time. I mention this not to in any way rush your design, but just to present the facts." HCPSr to FLW, 19 August 1952. FLWA.

29 HCPSr to FLW, 19 August 1952. FLWA.

30 Joe Price, interview with George Goodwin, 10 April 1993. PTAC Archives. He recalled, "The concept was for the people who worked in the building to live there, and get up, you just go through and look out the window at people slugging through these snowstorms and the ice and the cars sliding, and you just have a nice peaceful spot."

31 On 16 September 1952, in response to Price's query the day before, Wright wrote to Harold C. Price, Sr., "Your preliminary sketches and plans are well underway and soon will be completed." FLWA microfiche no. P123E04. PTAC 2004.02.05.

of our Dad as a normal everyday father but in reality he was a pioneer in his own business. Both Wright and my father had the pioneer spirit. They were both very loyal, patriotic men, immersed in the American culture. They had a wonderful rapport. Joe and I didn't have to do anything to encourage Dad to build the building. He was quite excited about it, and approved the initial concept." A rendering of such a sixteen story version of the design shows the building from the west. The southwest quadrant is apartments, with their continuous vertical fins and projecting balconies. Soon after this preliminary approval, Wright called Harold, Sr., and said, "It really needs to be higher….To get the space you want and all that, we need to go up. Is there any way we can go to nineteen stories?"[32] The final design for the Price Tower developed by the spring of 1953 did rise to nineteen stories above the ground.

The Price Tower's vertical élan closed with the copper-clad "light needle" that rose from the seventeenth-floor terrace on the edge of the north structural pier, to which the spire is anchored by horizontal steel rods. Its total height of seventy feet included thirty-five feet above this pier's top. Described at the tower's completion as a "television spire," the pole was not so equipped, although a radio transmission antenna was later attached. Price had borne without question the expense of the spire, which made his structure (at 221 feet) taller than its nearest rival, the 219-foot tower of the original Phillips Building of 1928.[33] After meeting Wright at Bartlesville in late October, Harold, Sr., confirmed to Wright that they had concluded that "the general design of the tower and the penthouse area will remain the same, with the possibility that we will add two more floors to the main portion of the tower," adding that "the general design of the elevation and the plan of the building is satisfactory to us."[34] For Price, the final decision about the number of stories depended on applicants for office space and apartments, interior sketches of which he requested from Wright, who was to design the furniture for Harold, Sr.'s office and for these rental areas, if requested to do so by the tenants.

Wright and his apprentices continued to prepare presentation and working drawings of the Price Tower through the winter of 1952-53 at Taliesin West. Both he and the Price Company were mindful of publicizing the design, nationally and regionally. By this time the design was called the Price Tower. Harold Price, Jr., recalled, "My Dad wanted it named that. We tried to get him to call it the Crystal Tower or something else to get our name off of it, but he really wanted it."[35]

The idea of the tower rising from a sea of greenery was consistent with Wright's metaphor for it as "the tree that escaped the crowded forest," and with the fact that Bartlesville's center was then still largely tree-lined like the rolling hills in which it was situated. As Joe Price recalled, apart from commercial blocks near the Phillips and Adams buildings, and the local church spires, "nothing was really more than one or two stories. When you were in the tower looking out, if you look out over the residential area, you could not see houses. It was just all trees, these big Dutch elms."[36] With its deep green color, the tower would both stand like a natural object when seen from far away and frame vistas of green countryside, since

32 HCPJr, interview with Sue Lacey, 24 February 1990, 3. PTAC Archives. Elsewhere he recalled that when they returned to Taliesin in October to see the design, Wright "had a picture, had a drawing of the then sixteen-story building and Dad just fell in love with it right away." HCPJr, interview with George M. Goodwin, 10 April 1993. PTAC Archives.

33 William Wesley Peters to Haskell Culwell, 12 April 1955, wrote, "Regarding the light needle on top of Tower building Mr. Wright and Mr. Price have decided to proceed with it as presently designed." FLWA, microfiche no. P141B10. The design as built featured lights set in tubular shell of copper through the needle's height. Joe Price to FLW, 27 September 1955, wrote "If someone would have been here, I am sure the television aerial would not have been placed where it is." FLWA, microfiche no. P143D10. Wesley Peters recalled that the spire "was decorative. Also, it was supposed to mark the tower in case of a low-flying airplane but that whole tower wasn't as high by any means. It was higher than the original Phillips building and Mr. Price commented on that and Mr. Wright said he could make it tall enough. But they used the excuse that it would be for an airplane beacon but I think I'm sure he really just wanted to use it that way…[Price] didn't anticipate building such a tall tower as that but I think he got accustomed to it because he was proud that it was commanding much more notoriety or attention than the Phillips buildings were." William Wesley Peters, interview with Greg Williams and Sue Lacey, 27 February 1990, 22,23. HCPJr recalled, "It was a decorative antenna to begin with. Then we attached the radio, the FM station's transmission antenna to it. It's a modified design but it was Wright's design and Wright's modification and it has no function other than artistic." HCPJr, interview with Sue Lacey, 24 February 1990, 16. PTAC Archives. The FM radio station that broadcast from the tower was KCBW, operated from the fall of 1961 by a couple from Kansas City who, for their first year in town, lived in the

Figure 2.10   Price Tower, model of 1953, at H. C. Price Co. booth, Oklahoma Building, International Petroleum Exposition, Tulsa, 14-23 May 1953, with (left to right), Joe D. Price, Mary Lou Price, Harold C. Price, Sr., and Harold C. Price, Jr. PTAC Archives.

Figure 2.11   Price Tower, model of 1953 showing electrically lit interiors, grounds, and rooftop. Photograph gift of Carolyn S. Price (PTAC 2004.12.3).

seventh- and eighth-floor apartment. Erna Wolcott-Conaster, interview with Arn Henderson and Sue Lacey, 22 August 1990. PTAC Archives. Wright, **Story of the Tower**, 102, described the light pole as a "television spire" seventy feet high. Culwell recalled, "that spire on the top, that was all added later. We were ninety-five percent finished with the building when they added that spire on the top of the building again, that thing wasn't cheap. It's all copper and Mr. Price didn't bat an eye—'Do it.' It's useless but it does look nice." Haskell Culwell, interview with Sue Lacey, 3 August 1990, 22. PTAC Archives.

34 HCPSr to FLW, 27 October 1952. PTAC Archives.

35 HCPJr, interview with George M. Goodwin, 10 April 1993. PTAC Archives.

36 Joe Price, interview with George M. Goodwin, 10 April 1993. PTAC Archives.

"its upper floors will command an unbroken view of all directions over eight hundred square miles of prairie and foothills."[37] To complete his tower's integration with the landscape, Wright planned a reflecting pool to its east, "which will serve as a mirror for the soaring grace of the Tower."[38] The Price Tower would thus fulfill his ideal of the singular skyscraper casting its shadow on its own land.

The most telling demonstration of Wright's design was the model of the Price Tower, unveiled at the International Petroleum Exposition in Tulsa of 14-23 May 1953 (Fig. 2.10). The event drew 250,000, among whom were company executives and independent oil producers who were Price's clients. To attract them to the Price Company's booth in the Oklahoma Building, as one of many exhibits in many buildings, Price announced the project regionally and sought national publicity as well. Wright himself attended the fair and appeared with Price at the exhibited model.[39] Wright requested that this model, begun toward the end of February 1953, have a scale of three eighths of an inch equaling one foot, so that the 186-foot tower would stand about six feet high. This model was illuminated from within to simulate the tower's nighttime appearance, and at its top was a tapering spire, emerging from the tower's center (Fig. 2.11). Lit from base to crown, the Price Tower compares with its region's oil rigs, whose nighttime lighting bedecked their tall skeletal frames. This image of the tower recalled the Exposition's publicity, which included towers for oil drilling equipment for sale. At night, these lit towers dominated the fairgrounds near Tulsa's electrically lit downtown skyscrapers.[40]

The theme of electrification was also an emblem of the Public Service Company of Oklahoma, whose Bartlesville offices with their separate entrance were to be located in the long horizontal wing of the tower's two-story base. These offices were served by a tunnel-like drive with windows along the sides for customers to pay their bills without leaving their cars, as shown on the tower's original site plan (Fig. 2.12). The Public Service Co.'s offices included a small auditorium designed to demonstrate the benefits of electrical home appliances.[41] The base was also to contain two floors of rental space for small shops entered off the north office lobby. There would be a separate entrance for the apartments on the south leading to the south elevator. Both the north and south entrances would have their own automobile courts with sheltered parking. This site plan was made possible by the Prices' acquisition of an additional lot north of the tower in March 1953. This provided parking for eight cars and, important to Wright, it "would add spaciousness to the entrance court and give more stance to the tower building."[42] The integration of sheltered parking places all around the base was a feature of the site plan which would distinguish the Price Tower from urban skyscrapers. Cars could drive past the north entrance to the offices, turn right through the driveway between the tower and the Public Services Company's offices, and then exit near the site's southeast corner. As Wright said of the parking area, "And the expansion at the ground greatly helps make our building appropriate to big town ground

37 "Frank Lloyd Wright's Concrete and Copper Skyscraper on the Prairie for H.C. Price Co.," **Architectural Forum** 98 (May 1953): 101.

38 Wright, **Story of the Tower**, 37. The reflecting pool appears in several studies for the Price Tower's site plan, including FLWA, drawings no. 5215.024, 5215.036, 5215.042, 5215.230, 5215.231, and 5215.232.

39 HCPSr to FLW, 2 April 1953. FLWA, microfiche no. P127A07. On Wright and Price appearing with the model, see "Price Tower Going Up," **Public Service News** (June 1953), back cover. Conoco-Phillips Archives, Bartlesville.

40 The built tower created a similar impression, "Because of the lavish use of glass, the tower gives off a warm, glowing light after dark to the downtown areas. Approaching the city from a distance, we found the tower appeared like a slender finger of light pointing toward the sky." Rainey Heard Williams, "Interior Is Divided into Quadrants," **Christian Science Monitor**, 30 March 1956. Wright's scale for the model was noted in Besinger, **Working with Mr. Wright**, 249. The model "was an exact replica of the 18-story tower on which construction is expected to start June 1. Built by Wright's staff, the model is six feet, four inches high and stands on a four-foot base. Interior and spot lighting will reflect the advanced architectural features and the brilliant design of the new building." The Price Co. exhibit also featured "a large modernistic plastic map bearing the route of many of the nation's principal pipe lines and indicating those portions constructed by HCPCO during its thirty years of pipelining." Price Co. pipe coating products were displayed, and Harold Price, Sr., HCPJr and other company officials were at the exhibit to greet visitors. "Price Tower Model Shown," **Tulsa Daily World**, 14 May 1953, International Petroleum Exposition Edition, sec. 1, pt. 2, p. 5. The model, which took 410 man hours to build, was mainly assembled by Eric Lloyd Wright, with assistance from Taliesin apprentices Kenn Lockhart and Kamal [El Din?]. It included balsa wood furnishings, brass door jambs and furniture, and copper ornament. "Model for the H.C. Price Company; Expenses," 29 January 1954. PTAC Archives. After its display in Tulsa, the model was shown in New York in June-July 1953.

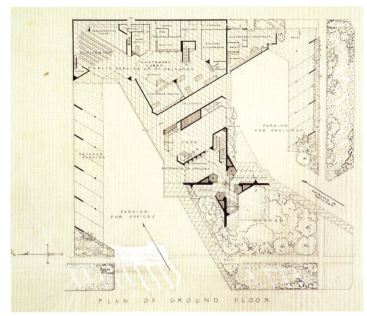

PLAN OF GROUND FLOOR

Figure 2.12 (Catalogue No. 25). Price Tower, Bartlesville, Oklahoma, 1952-1956. Ground floor plan, showing spaces for Public Service Company of Oklahoma northeast of tower, with parking for dwellings (south) and offices (north). Driveway between retail shop and Public Service Co. was subsequently enclosed. FLWF 5215.014. © Frank Lloyd Wright Foundation.

instead of overgrown cities."[43] Architectural control over the automobile was a key premise of his late works, from Usonian houses to large public structures. As he said to his apprentices in 1958, "you should start with the parking, not do the building and then try to find the parking—but get the parking and then do the building."[44]

Redesigning and Building the Price Tower

Wright's apprentices completed working drawings and specifications of the Price Tower in mid-April 1953, and Price invited six contractors to Bartlesville to submit proposals.[45] Yet Wright replied that inviting at most three likely candidates would suffice, "in as much as only a few men [are] fit to build this building."[46] Price wrote that, of the five firms that gave preliminary estimates, the relatively small Culwell Construction Co. of Oklahoma City had "done some of the finer buildings for the University of Oklahoma at Norman, and was suggested and very well recommended by Bruce Goff."[47] Haskell Culwell (b. 1907) had started as a mason to become a masonry contractor and then a general contractor. His firm was then working on the university's Home Economics Building. Impressed with Culwell's work on this unusual structure, Goff recommended to Wright that Culwell's bid be solicited for the Price Tower, and Culwell conferred with Wright and Price, and had several talks with Wesley Peters to determine methods of building Wright's design, before he submitted his estimate.[48]

HCPSr to FLW, 8 June 1953, wrote, "you had the model on exhibit in New York for two months, and, therefore, in all probability it would not be available early in July." FLWA, microfiche no. P129B04. The model appeared at the exhibition of Wright's life's work at the pavilion on the site of the future Guggenheim Museum in New York. "Frank Lloyd Wright Show Opens," **New York Herald Tribune**, 23 October 1953. Bruce Goff wished to exhibit the model at the University of Oklahoma's School of Architecture. Bruce Goff to HCPSr, 6 August 1953. FLWA, microfiche no. P130E01. A similar request came from the chapter of Tau Sigma Delta, the national honor society of architecture, at the University of Kansas. Thomas Wellman to HCPSr, 18 October 1954. FLWA, microfiche no. P130A03. The model was included in an exhibit of Wright's work at the University of Wisconsin, Madison, October-November 1955. Eugene Masselink to HCPSr, 26 September 1955. FLWA, microfiche no. P143D07.

41 "Price Tower Plans Announced." **Tie-In** (Spring 1953): 3. PTAC Archives. Besinger, **Working with Mr. Wright**, 242, recalled. "An office block, which was to be occupied by the public service company, was pulled away from the base of the tower and placed at one side of the site. This gave their offices a separate entrance and a separate identity." See also "Public Service Has Moved to Price Tower," **Public Service News** (February 1956): 2-6.

42 FLW to HCPSr, 23 March 1953. FLWA, microfiche no. P126E07.

43 FLW to HCPSr, 4 February 1956. FLWA, microfiche no. P147C08, PTAC 2004.02.52a.

44 Wright, "Gammage Auditorium and Greek Orthodox Church," talk to Taliesin Fellows, 14 December 1958, in **Frank Lloyd Wright: His Living Voice**, ed. Bruce Brooks Pfeiffer (Fresno: The Press at California State University, 1987), 53.

45 HCPSr to FLW, 6 April 1953. FLWA, microfiche no. P127A10. Working with Price in this period was a building committee: Elmer L. Gallery, vice president and treasurer; J. Stewart Dewar, vice-president of the somastic division; Alton Rowland, counselor; and Harold C. Price., Jr., administrative assistant. "Bartlesville Firm to Build Skyscraper," **Tulsa World**, 8 May 1953.

46 FLW to HCPSr, 17 April 1953. FLWA, microfiche no. P127C10, PTAC 2004.02.13.

47 HCPSr to FLW, 20 April 1953. FLWA, microfiche no. P127D03.

48 Haskell Culwell, interview with Sue Lacey, 3 August 1990, 1. PTAC Archives.

Figure 2.13 Mary Lou Price, Harold C. Price, Sr., Frank Lloyd Wright, and Harold C. Price, Jr., with plans of the Price Tower. Photograph by Joe Price (PTAC 2003.16.003).

The process of preparing the design for realization involved a long series of three-way negotiations between Wright, the Prices, and Culwell (Fig. 2.13). The publicity surrounding the project's unveiling included a feature article in *Architectural Forum* of May 1953, which claimed that the tower "will probably be the costliest office building ever erected."[49] The editor claimed that this assessment was not based on access to contractors' estimates, yet the three firms that were finalists for the job produced estimates that averaged just over $2,000,000, over twice the maximum of $1,000,000 that the Prices had wanted to spend and that Wright had originally estimated as the maximum total cost.[50] With these bids in hand, Harold Price, Sr., wrote to Wright that, given rentable space within the building's area of 60,000 square feet, the maximum annual rental income would be $150,000. For the project to be economically viable, the building's cost including the land could total no more than $1,500,000, the maximum figure supportable by the rental income. For that total cost, the maximum rental income could just pay operating expenses, depreciation, taxes, and insurance, but no interest on the investment. Thus the Price Company could not initially contemplate a project whose costs totaled more than $1,500,000. Price told Wright, "You think it can be done for that and I hope it can be done for less."[51]

With this hope the Prices went ahead with awarding the contract to the lowest bidder, Haskell Culwell, whose figure of $1,766,000 the Prices and Wright sought to bring down once subcontractors and suppliers were provided with working drawings for estimating. This was a leap of faith on the part of a client who had originally sought a low building to cost no more than $750,000 payable out of the company's resources. Culwell's figure amounted to a cost of $31.50 per square foot at a time when the Prices understood first-rate construction to cost $20.00 per square foot. The tower's unusual geometry and construction made it difficult to estimate costs. Culwell recalled, "We couldn't believe it would ever be built. It was just too extreme and too advanced in design when we first were asked to bid on it. One of our first problems was that of materials. Prices were hard to get from suppliers. It was hard to know ourselves what we would need."[52] Wright maintained that his unique architecture would cost no more than conventional building, but the Prices' resources were not unlimited. As Harold, Jr., recalled, "Wright worked diligently to cut the costs. The original plan had a much more complicated air conditioning system, and a much more complicated construction system...We modified the structure to reduce the costs. And Wright worked for a long time on that."[53]

49 "Frank Lloyd Wright's Concrete and Copper Skyscraper on the Prairie," **Architectural Forum** 98 (May 1953): 102. HCPSr to FLW, 5 June 1953, wrote, "I am not worrying any more about the article in the FORUM. I doubt if it will have any effect on the cost of the building. Besides, the article should influence reputable contractors and subcontractors in their desire to participate in the construction. I don't think any of the contractors with whom we were dealing gave those figures to [editor/publisher Perry I.] Prentice. He says they did not. They probably obtained the estimate from a New York contractor to whom they showed the structural design. The ridiculous figure of $300,000 for the concrete seems to prove this." FLWA, microfiche no. P129A07, PTAC 2004.02.25. Similar facts appeared in **Forum**'s parent publication: "When the Price Tower is completed, in about a year, at an estimated cost of $1,500,000, it may well be the costliest building, foot for foot, ever erected in the U.S." "Real Estate; Prairie Skyscraper," **Time**, 25 May 1953, 94.

50 Price Tower; Approximate Cost Estimates, 23 June 1953. The three finalists' bids were those of Haskell Culwell, Oklahoma City ($1,766,000); D.A. Harmon, Oklahoma City ($2,002,000); and Robert W. Long, Kansas City ($2,245,000). PTAC 2004.02.28.

51 HCPSr to FLW, 25 June 1953. FLWA, microfiche no. P129D07, PTAC 2004.02.28.

52 Culwell quoted in "Skyscraper Cast Its Shadow on the Plains," **Business Week**, 18 February 1956, 116.

53 HCPJr, interview with George M. Goodwin, 10 April 1993. PTAC Archives. HCPSr to FLW, 15 July 1953, wrote, "I am pleased to hear that so much was being done to simplify the frame of the building and arrangement of the facilities. We will await your drawing to see how this has been accomplished." FLWA, microfiche no. P130B01, PTAC Archives. Haskell Culwell recalled of Wright, "We never worked with any architect that we thought was any nicer to work with. And the stories that you hear and I've heard over the years about how hard he is to work with. We never found him any more unreasonable than any architect. Most of the time, he was easy going. You could never say 'can't be done' or 'won't be done' or this to him. You could always reason with him and he would listen to reason, like the light fixtures and structural things....Like the first meeting I had with Mr. Wright on the Price Tower, I forget now what it was, but he said, 'You can build that building much cheaper than that. Let's figure out how we can do it cheaper.' We sat down, Mr. Wright and Wes and I, and we had different ideas and everything and finally we'd get through but we'd end up about the same price we'd started with. He finally agreed that that would be probably as cheap as you could ever build that building." Haskell Culwell, interview with Sue Lacey, 3 August 1990, 26. PTAC Archives.

Wright's main collaborators on the tower were Peters, who was both an engineer and supervising architect on the site, and Mendel Glickman (1895-1967), as the structural engineer, who was at the University of Oklahoma but who worked in summers and part-time at Taliesin.[54] As a consultant for mechanical engineering, Wright hired Samuel R. Lewis of Chicago, who worked with Glickman to integrate the structural and mechanical systems. In Wright's view, all of these consultants should be paid by the architect from his total fee and not paid separately by the client. Although this approach was costly for the architect, Wright favored it because it enabled him to co-ordinate decisions about structural and mechanical features so as to serve his architectural aims.[55] All minds worked through the summer of 1953 to simplify the structural frame and spatial arrangement. Originally the Prices had hoped to begin the building in June and to complete it by summer 1954. Yet redesign delayed the start of construction until November 1953, prior to which the streets at the site were widened and overhead utility lines were transferred to underground conduits. Wright had "insisted the overhead wires be removed to permit the unique building to stand clean and uncluttered."[56]

Regarding oversight of the project during construction, Wright wrote to Harold Price, Sr., as the tower neared completion that "In this case I took this superintendent to be Joe [Price]. While inexperienced I felt his love for the building project would make up for that and the extra work would not be too much for us. This assumption has been alright as far as your architect is concerned."[57] During the course of the tower's construction, Joe Price, then a much practiced amateur photographer, took thousands of photographs documenting the process from start to finish. The photographs were meant to become a film on Wright, which Joe Price tried to create from a series of still images taken from fixed vantage points each day around the tower as it rose. Though it was ultimately an unworkable concept, given daily changes in weather conditions, and in the visibility of different sections as their formwork was set and poured, this film was "all built on the tower as it

54 Peters recalled of the Price Tower's engineering, "Mendel Glickman and I both worked on it. Originally, Mendel Glickman was working with me and we worked together on the basic typical floor patterns the way they were going to be….He was always very helpful in solving a very difficult problem. There weren't so many difficult problems but I would say Mendel also designed a large part of the mechanical system although there [were] some other consultants involved in that." William Wesley Peters, interview with Gregory Williams and Sue Lacey, 27 February 1990, 4. PTAC Archives. Culwell's subcontractors were W.A. Flanders, Oklahoma City, for plumbing and heating; Industrial Electric, Oklahoma City; and Standard Roofing and Sheet Metal, Oklahoma City and Ponca City, who set the fins or vanes on the walls and welded the ornamental and non-ornamental copper panels onto the concrete. Culwell recalled that he was on the site about one day per week, and that Wesley Peters was there typically once a month. Culwell was then also building the Price house in Phoenix and the HCPJr house in Bartlesville, and he often stayed at Taliesin West when conferring with Wright's staff on these jobs. On site from start to finish were Haskell's foreman Bill Donnell and engineer Jack Cook. Haskell Culwell, interview with Sue Lacey, Bartlesville, 3 August 1990, 3, 5. PTAC Archives. Wright himself visited the site six to eight times during construction, from June 1953 to February 1956, usually en route between Taliesin and Taliesin West. Yet Price did express concern about the infrequency of his visits, writing, "The twelfth floor of our building will be poured sometime next week. Because this building was basically designed by you twenty-five years ago, and now is finally materializing, we felt sure that you would give it your best, personal attention. You were last in Bartlesville, on January 7th, of this year—before the building was above ground. You have not seen it since. We are all astounded and quite hurt that you seem so little interest [sic] in the building, itself, and that you place its consideration after your newer projects and exhibits." HCPSr to FLW, 22 October 1954. FLWA, microfiche no. P138B01.

55 FLW to HCPSr, 27 March 1956, wrote, "The fee is finally reckoned as one on all construction, furnishing and planting. Usually there are separate fees for engineering, air-conditioning, furniture, decorations and planting. I found long ago that the only way superior results could be had was by the architect covering the entire matter to the best of his ability. This has proved immensely difficult and expensive to him beyond anything covered by his construction fee." FLWA, microfiche no. P148B09. Wright later wrote to Price, "You probably do not know that my fees at 10% cost straight for all five services: Building, Engineering, Furnishing, Planting and Decoration are not much above half the average first-class architect's fee if all these fees are added?" FLW to HCPSr, 3 September 1956. FLWA, microfiche no. P150D07.

56 "October to See Start of Price Tower," **Tulsa Tribune**, 1 October 1953. Intended construction time (June 1953 to summer 1954) was noted in "Tower to Provide Office, Living Space," **Engineering-News Record** (4 June 1953): 23; and "Price Tower Will Be Built in Bartlesville," **Construction News Monthly** (10 June 1953): 117-18. Among changes requested in the plans, Harold C. Price, Sr., wrote to Wright, "The people who will be using the apartments are the type who would greatly prefer two separate baths, but as there does not seem to be room on the mezzanine floor the best we can do is provide a bathtub and a separate shower stall on the mezzanine floor. Would you please make an extra effort on this." HCPSr to FLW, 13 July 1953. FLWA, microfiche no. P130B01. Final plans did include a bathtub and shower on the mezzanine.

57 FLW to HCPSr, 28 December 1955. FLWA, microfiche no. P146A01. Wright wrote that "an architect does not superintend a building costing over $100,000.00. He supervises a superintendent only. That superintendent is duly appointed satisfactory to both architect and owner and is paid by the owner." On Joe Price's role in the construction, Culwell recalled, "He was just there, looking after his Dad's interest more or less…. He stayed there pretty well all day through the construction of it." Haskell Culwell, interview with Sue Lacey, 3 August 1990, 5, 6. PTAC Archives. Joe Price wrote to Wright, "This is the first time I have been labeled superintendent. I have been working for and paid by Haskell Culwell, making any superintending difficult. As for being inexperienced, how can I ever tell you what you want when I have trouble knowing even what I want." Joe Price to FLW, 2 January 1956. FLWA, microfiche no. P147A01.

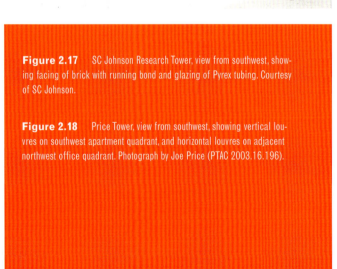

Figure 2.17 SC Johnson Research Tower, view from southwest, showing facing of brick with running bond and glazing of Pyrex tubing. Courtesy of SC Johnson.

Figure 2.18 Price Tower, view from southwest, showing vertical louvres on southwest apartment quadrant, and horizontal louvres on adjacent northwest office quadrant. Photograph by Joe Price (PTAC 2003.16.196).

63 Pouring the top nineteenth floor was noted in HCPSr to FLW, 15 January 1955. FLWA, microfiche no. P140A09. Reference to the strike appeared in William Wesley Peters to Haskell Culwell, 22 January 1954, FLWA, microfiche no. P133A08; Peters to Harold C. Price., Jr., 24 February 1954, FLWA, microfiche no. P133E08; HCPJr to FLW, 13 March 1954, FLWA, microfiche no. P134A08; HCPSr to FLW, 17 May 1954, FLWA, microfiche no. P135A03. By July 1955 all concrete had been poured and the windows installed, but a sheet-metal workers' strike delayed installation of exterior louvres. "Completion Set This Year," **Tulsa Daily World**, 10 July 1955.

64 HCPJr, telephone conversation with author, 20 July 2004.

would not attract more traditional lenders or investors. By contrast, it had been the spatial and structural unconventionality of the St. Mark's Tower of 1929 that had discouraged potential lenders from supporting its realization.

Despite a ten-week metalworkers strike from January to March 1954, the Price Tower's skeletal structure had topped out through the nineteenth floor by January 1955.[63] Externally the major task through the spring of 1955 was placing the aluminum window frames and copper spandrel panels, vertical copper fins, and horizontal copper louvres.[64] There was concern that rain water dripping off the copper would stain and discolor the aluminum, but Wright replied, "I am not sure the discoloring of the aluminum isn't a happy circumstance."[65] The building was to be finished in October, though there was still little furniture. By 21 September Joe Price wrote to Wright that "the louvers are half way [sic] down on the apartments and north side. The effect is tremendous."[66] Joe Price called for Wright to come to Bartlesville to help assess the building's completion, but Wright replied, "Before I can be of much real help (besides reassuring you) the whole fabric should be pretty much together. Then I can judge and recommend the slight measures that will tune the fiddle. This is always the case."[67]

As completed the Price Tower stood with its accentuated verticality almost wholly isolated in its immediate surroundings. Partly for this reason, the building looks taller than its nineteen floors, because there are no adjacent towers with which the eye can compare it. Because it is visible from all sides, and because it is planned on an angle with respect to the surrounding street grid, the tower's varied faces look more animated than a conventional tall building foursquare to the street and with similar façades. Unlike such structures, the Price Tower has no single front or privileged elevation. It can hardly be said to have a façade in the traditional sense, given the interweaving of its quadrants. What is inarguable is the tower's insistent visual verticality and tautness. This effect derives from many decisions, but perhaps the most important of them is that the major horizontals stop at the sixteenth floor's roof terrace, while the four core vertical fins and the exterior northeast stair tower rise to the top, with the light needle extending the whole tower's asymmetrical profile into the sky. As Wright wrote to Mary Lou Price shortly after the building opened, "the great upraised hand proclaims beauty for Bartlesville."[68] Like an upraised hand, whose fingers form a stepped, asymmetrical silhouette, so the profile of the Price Tower varies with the viewpoint of the observer around its base. The tower's verticality is most accentuated when viewed from the west, where the fins rising through the apartment quadrant reinforce a perception of slenderness. The result is to make the tower a spire-like landmark amidst the town's older church spires (Fig. 2.18).

65 FLW to Haskell Culwell, 25 February 1955, FLWA, microfiche no. P140D04. Wright added, "There is no cure except a lacquer with the final color of the copper in it. This may not be necessary. We will watch to see." Concern for discoloration of the copper recurred in Jerry G. Spann, Bissell Builders Supply Co, to Haskell Culwell, 11 November 1954, FLWA, microfiche no. P138C08; and Culwell to FLW, 14 February 1955, FLWA, microfiche no. P140C09.

66 Joe Price to FLW, 21 September 1955. FLWA, microfiche no. P143D04. HCPSr to FLW, 2 September 1955, wrote, "We hope to have the building completed by the end of October, and unless we finally get the furniture designs accepted by all parties and start manufacture of same within the next week, it looks as if we will be in the building with the same furniture we have in our present offices." FLWA, microfiche no. P143C03.

67 FLW to Joe Price, 29 September 1955. FLWA, microfiche no. P143E05.

68 FLW to Mary Lou Price, 9 March 1956. FLWA, microfiche no. P148A09. Wright here echoed part of the passage inscribed on the lobby wall that he had adapted from Walt Whitman's *Leaves of Grass* and to which he added some of his own sentences. HCPJr, interview with Sue Lacey, 24 February 1990, 18-19. PTAC Archives. The lobby mural reads in capital letters [brackets indicate sources in Whitman's *Leaves of Grass*, third edition of 1860]: "TOWARD ALL/I RAISE HIGH THE PERPENDICULAR HAND. I MAKE THE SIGNAL/TO REMAIN AFTER ME IN SIGHT FOREVER/FOR ALL THE HAUNTS AND HOMES OF MEN. ["Salut au Monde!," closing verse 37]..........WHERE THE CITY OF THE FAITHFULLEST FRIENDS STANDS [Chants Democratic 2: "Song of the Broad-Axe," verse 10, line 18] /WHERE THRIFT IS IN ITS PLACE BUT PRUDENCE IS IN ITS PLACE ["Song of the Broad-Axe." verse 10, line 5: "Where thrift is in its place, and prudence is in its place,"] /WHERE BEHAVIOR IS THE FINEST OF THE FINE ARTS ["Song of the Broad-Axe," verse 10, line 6]/WHERE OUTSIDE AUTHORITY ENTERS ALWAYS AFTER THE/PRECEDENCE OF INSIDE AUTHORITY ["Song of the Broad-Axe," verse 8, line 1]/WHERE THE CITY THAT HAS PRODUCED THE GREATEST MAN STANDS ["Song of the Broad-Axe," verse 8, line 1: "The greatest city is that which has the greatest man or woman."] /THERE THE GREATEST CITY STANDS. ["Song of the Broad-Axe," verse 10, line 22.] /WALT WHITMAN 1860." See Edwin Harold Eby, ed., **A Concordance of Walt Whitman's Leaves of Grass and Selected Prose Writings** (Seattle: University of Washington Press, 1955); and **Walt Whitman's Blue Book: 1860-61** *Leaves of Grass* Containing His Manuscript Additions and Revisions, 2 vols. (New York: The New York Public Library, 1968).

Early Criticism and Response

Perhaps no tall building of the 1950s in the United States received more critical attention than the Price Tower after it opened in February 1956. As Wright's only tall office or apartment building, the structure was widely reviewed in both the architectural and popular press. Among the initial accounts was a particularly critical article that appeared in *Business Week* that identified the building as the world's most modern office structure—and the most expensive per square foot. The article implied that Wright's design had been accepted by the Prices without their understanding its costs of construction and operation. In response Harold Price, Sr., wrote to the editor, "If the inaccuracies and seemingly derogatory statements affected only our Company, I would disregard the matter entirely. But I cannot refrain from calling to your attention to what I consider a most unfair attitude toward Mr. Frank Lloyd Wright and also toward the city of Bartlesville.... It is also intimated that I and the officers of my Company are dissatisfied with the building. Nothing could be further from the truth. Your reporter asked me that question in my office and I told him in front of others that we were very proud of the building and thoroughly satisfied with Mr. Wright's design."[69]

Price first had asked for a building of 25,000 square feet to cost $700,000. He recalled that Wright "assured us that a building could be built for $20.00 per square foot, and we based all our calculations of rental, etc. upon that figure. We decided to add apartments and increase the footage to 50,000 square feet with an expenditure of $1,000,000.00. We finally raised this to $1,250,000.00, exclusive of the architect's fee, and you insisted that it could be done for that amount. The final figure, exclusive of the architect's fee, amounted to approximately $2,100,000.00. Nothing had been added to the building we originally contemplated except the necessary changes to make corrections in the original design and engineering and to make a completed structure." The tower's cost, combined with that of the Price house in Phoenix ($228,000) and the Harold Price, Jr., house in Bartlesville ($229,000), exclusive of architects' fees, had "placed an embarrassing strain on both the company and the family. It has been necessary for the company to extend its borrowings from the banks for current operations to a much greater extent than usual, and has prevented us from expansion in needed equipment." Yet Price reported to Wright that "all of us in the family are very happy with The Tower and both houses."[70]

As completed the tower had a gross footage of 57,315 square feet and a net rental footage of 42,000 square feet. Each upper floor contained about 1,900 gross square feet, including 1,150 square feet of rentable office space, while each two-story apartment had 982 square feet. The building's cost was $35.55 per square foot, or $52.00 per rentable square foot. When dedicated in March 1956, about half the office space was rented. The small northeast quadrant (280 square feet) cost $135

69 HCPSr to Elliott V. Bell, Editor and Publisher, **Business Week**, 25 February 1956. FLWA, microfiche no. P147D09. Wright was quite upset at the article, writing to Price, "Beware of the envious. We are where envy will come our way. Regarding 'Business Week'—slander in its worst form. A reporter, instead of factual reporting handing in hearsay." Wright contemplated suing the magazine for damages to investment and reputation. FLW to HCPSr., 29 February 1956, FLWA, microfiche no. P148A03. Wright soon discussed the Price Tower on television with Tex McCrary on 23 April 1956, PTAC 2004.02.55, and on the Will Rogers and Monitor programs. Kenneth S. Adams to HCPSr, 3 May 1956, PTAC 2004.02.56; HCPSr to FLW, 4 May 1956, FLWA, microfiche no. P148E10, PTAC 2004.02.58; FLW to HCPSr, 11 May 1956, FLWA, microfiche no. P149A01; and HCPSr to FLW, 14 May 1956, FLWA microfiche no. S254E03. PTAC 2004.02.59. Culwell confirmed that Price supported the project all the way, "I probably, in all my years of construction, I never ran across a nicer, more agreeable man than Mr. Price. He was just unbelievable. I don't think he ever wanted to waste a dime but if it made the building prettier or better, he was for it. I mean, he never, I don't think he ever complained about the costs. Whatever Mr. Wright wanted, Mr. Price would go along with it with never any talk of what the cost was going to be, he'd never ask. He'd just say, 'Do it.'" Haskell Culwell, interview with Sue Lacey, 3 August 1990, 25. PTAC Archives.

70 HCPSr to FLW, 30 August 1956. FLWA, microfiche no. P150C09.

71 Ibid. Peters recalled that Mies van der Rohe's Seagram Building in New York (1954-58) cost $85.00 per square foot, and "it was considered the biggest cost of any office building that had been built in New York. The Guggenheim Museum cost somewhere in the 30's—I don't remember if it was $32." William Wesley Peters, interview with Gregory Williams and Sue Lacey, 27 February 1990, 15. PTAC Archives. HCPJr recalled that the apartments rented for $135 per month, which was too expensive, "so one by one the apartments were converted into offices...they worked very well at that. The building filled up. People came in, nobody left. Any tenant we had liked it. We were charging the top rate that we could for the area, six or seven dollars a square foot, not that much to begin with, but as time went on the doctors and lawyers started moving in and they liked the space." HCPJr, interview with George M. Goodwin, 10 April 1993. PTAC Archives. Initial rental figures were noted in "Skyscraper Cast Its Shadow on the Plains," **Business Week**, 18 February 1956, 118.

72 Werner Moser flew from Cambridge, Massachusetts, to Tulsa on 29 May 1956. FLW to HCPSr, May 1956. FLWA.

per month, while the northwest and southeast quadrants (c. 440 square feet) rented for $185 per month. For the apartments, apart from the topmost one for the
Price family, rent was $325 per month, with architect Bruce Goff as the only ini-
tial tenant. By August 1956 about two thirds of the space (c. 28,000 square feet)
had been rented at an average rate of about $3.40 per square foot annually, yield-
ing an annual income of $96,000 annually or $8,000 per month, with operating
costs of $9,000 per month. Once fully rented, the building would yield $12,000 per
month with operating costs of $10,000 per month, yielding a gross profit of
$24,000 per year, or one per cent of the building cost, not including depreciation.
The project was thus financially marginal, and Price reminded Wright, "We are
contractors and the publicity the building has evoked in no way increases our
business or income."[71]

If the tower did not contribute directly to the Price Company's success, it nevertheless did make its company famous outside its own industry. Given Wright's
worldwide reputation in the 1950s, initial interest in his Price Tower was international. In May 1956, Swiss architect Werner Moser, leader of the modern movement
in Switzerland and son of famed architect Karl Moser (1860-1936) of Basel, flew to
Bartlesville expressly to see the tower.[72] In 1956 the United States Information
Service wrote a feature story on the building for distribution to its missions
abroad as an explanation of American life and architecture. In 1957 Arthur Drexler
asked the Prices to permit their building to be exhibited at The Museum of Modern
Art, and W. Eugene Smith photographed the building for an exhibition at the
National Gallery of Art in Washington, D.C., Harold Price, Sr.'s native city.[73]
Presumably this attention helped to justify the company's investment in their
tower. As students, Michael Graves and Robert Beckley commented,
"Architecture is admittedly the costliest of the arts and the H.C. Price Company
will have to spend nearly three million dollars for Wright's structure. But is this so
absurd when a single television show can cost $100,000 and as soon as its allotted
hour is up lose all its advertising value?"[74] Not only did tourists from around the
world come to Bartlesville to see the tower, but overseas, where the company's
name was visible on its vehicles in the field, "people would come up to us actually
and say, 'Are you the company that has the Price Tower?' And these weren't
Americans, they were from Singapore and Brazil."[75]

H. C. Price Company occupied the tower from its opening in February 1956 to its
sale to the Phillips Company in 1981. During this period, accounts of employee-
occupants attest that the office interiors served the firm well, although the
building's unusual and experimental design also created unforeseen problems.
While the Price Tower's plans did increase usable area for offices and apartments
relative to the tower's total area, the module meant that all furniture had to be
unusually angular in design in order for this increase in usable area to be experi-

73 HCPSr to FLW, 11 December 1956, mentioned that he and Joe had conferred with Drexler at The Museum of Modern Art, where Drexler was then curator of architecture and design. FLWA, microfiche no. P151D08. Of Eugene Smith's photographing the tower for the National Gallery, Joe Price wrote to Wright on 17 December 1956, "The exhibition means a lot to my father. It is his home coming." FLWA, microfiche no. P151D10. PTAC Archives. The USIS feature, "Frank Lloyd Wright's First Skyscraper Soars over the American Prairie," was noted in Howard Needham to Richard Hoyt, H.C. Price Co., 15 August 1956. Conoco-Phillips Archives, Bartlesville. A Kansas City firm asked Price about building a duplicate of the tower, to which Price presumably would have objected, since his structure was intended to be the unique symbol of his company. HCPSr to William R. Stanley, 16 May 1956. PTAC Archives. Tulsa architect Malcolm L. McCune designed a pentagonal variant of the Price Tower as the Bel Air Towers apartments at 93rd and Nall Avenue in Kansas City. "Price Tower 'Twin' Planned for Kansas City," **Bartlesville Record**, 8 September 1955.

74 Michael Graves and Robert Beckley, "The H.C. Price Tower," **One Quarter Scale** [College of Applied Arts, University of Cincinnati] 3 (Winter 1955-1956): 15-16.

75 Bill Creel, interview with Sue Lacey and Arn Henderson, 21 August 1990, 6. PTAC Archives.

Figure 2.19 Dankmar Adler and Louis Sullivan, Guaranty Building, Buffalo, New York, 1894-96, from the northeast. Photograph by Ralph Cleveland.

enced in the interiors. Some in the Price Company used the angular Wright-designed desks set along the walls, yet others preferred familiar squared furnishings set out from the walls (as needed by some tenants such as doctors) and these would cause loss of living space.[76] While the tower withstood the buffeting of regional tornados, its original windows had a tendency to leak when pelted with wind-driven, gusty rains. In addition, while the quadrant design acoustically separated offices from each other, the hard materials within each office (concrete, glass, mahogany, steel) made for disturbing levels of noise. Finally, the copper louvers, although they did shield the glass from hot sun and sky glare, would get terribly hot in sunlight and the undersides of the louvers facing the windows would radiate heat into the building.[77] Manager Bill Creel recalled, "The worst part of the year was the summertime and, of course, if you had an office that caught the sun, it got awful hot and that's when you'd put your window units in. The women had fans by their desks. In the winter time…I think it was heated adequately except for the secretaries' section and that may have had to do with the doors opening and coming in. I know a lot of the secretaries had heaters, little heaters by their desks."[78] The elevators, custom designed by the Otis Elevator Company to fit their irregular hexagonal shafts, were Bartlesville's first automatic elevators and there were problems in getting people to use them.[79] With the south elevator for the apartments, the other three were adequate for daily operations, but they were too small for large furniture and equipment, which were hauled by pulley up the tower's exterior.[80]

Originally the Price Company's sixty employees in the tower occupied the four upper office floors (twelfth through fifteenth) below the sixteenth-floor roof garden and the company's set of executive offices (seventeenth through nineteenth). Other offices filled mainly with lawyers and doctors. Harold Price, Jr., recalled, "The building wasn't really accepted by the community as far as occupying the space. For many, many years we had a lot of space. But when we did have a tenant, they loved it. It was a good place to work."[81] The apartments were never fully rented, because of their cost and because units did not have enough closet space. At various times, Joe and Harold Price, Jr., stayed in the company's apartment on the seventeenth and eighteenth floors, and Bruce Goff rented the ninth- and tenth-floor apartment from 1956 through 1963, after which he moved his practice to Kansas City. Joe Price recalled that only five of the apartments were ever rented at one time. Tenants liked their units and had not found them to be too small, yet rents were high by local standards. In Bartlesville people preferred houses to apartments, and in 1960 Taliesin Architects drew plans for converting the apartments into offices.[82]

Years later, Joe Price assessed the building's value in terms of its effect on the working life of the company's employees. He admitted that in terms of rental income per square footage, the building did not pay. Yet he argued that "you have a terrible time when you try to judge a building by its balance sheet. Because on the balance sheet it never shows that the employees come in early and they leave late because it's so much more of a pleasure being there than being home. It doesn't show when you haven't had an employee leave you in thirty years…that the wait list of people wanting to work there is unlimited."[83] Bill Creel similarly recalled that

76 Ibid.

77 William Wesley Peters, interview with Gregory Williams and Sue Lacey, 27 February 1990, 15. PTAC Archives. Leakage was noted in "Skyscraper Cast Its Shadow on the Plains," **Business Week**, 18 February 1956, 117. One early apartment tenant recalled, "The only few inconveniences were that perhaps the heating and air conditioning didn't just work 100 percent and, of course, that the rain would come in. And we did have to have buckets and lots of rags handy when it happened. If the rain would come from a certain area, it would come in strong, like in buckets. If it came straight down, it was not so bad. But we could overlook those inconveniences, because it was elegant living. I must say, it really was." Erna Wolcott-Conatser, interview with Sue Lacey and Arn Henderson, 22 August 1990, 6. PTAC Archives.

78 Bill Creel, interview with Sue Lacey and Arn Henderson, 21 August 1990, 7. PTAC Archives.

79 HCPJr, interview with Sue Lacey, 24 February 1990, 9-10. PTAC Archives.

80 Bill Creel, interview with Sue Lacey and Arn Henderson, 21 August 1990, 12. PTAC Archives.

81 HCPJr, interview with Sue Lacey, 24 February 1990, 7. PTAC Archives.

82 Joe Price, interview with George M. Goodwin, 10 April 1993. PTAC Archives. On Goff's apartment, see "When the Designers Design for Themselves," **Architectural Forum** 117 (July 1962): 104-09, and De Long, **Bruce Goff**, 140, 324 n 2. The drawings for the remodeling of the apartments into offices are signed by William Wesley Peters and dated 1 March 1960. PTAC Archives. By the time the Price Co. sold the building to the Phillips Co. in 1981, all the apartments had been converted to offices except for the topmost one on the seventeenth and eighteenth floor, originally designed for the Price family and containing the "Blue Moon" mural executed by Wright.

83 Joe Price, interview with George M. Goodwin, 10 April 1993. PTAC Archives.

the tower's design and the company's management were mutually reinforcing, concluding, "In spite of the troubles with the slow elevators, the heating—I think everybody who was working in the building liked the building. You didn't hear a lot of complaints, 'Oh, I wish we'd go move somewhere else.' We enjoyed it and it is always kind of hard, I think, when you are in a building like this that is so novel and so different, to know how much of an effect on your corporate psychology, or character, or whatever you want to call it, is due to the building and the environment you have and how much is due to the people that are actually running and motivating. But we had, several of us still maintain, the finest corporation there ever was in existence. We never had trouble trying to find people to work, never had trouble with people leaving. It was a wonderful place to work, the company was, of course. That flowed into the tower and the tower, I think, helped make the people here like it because it was a very relaxed atmosphere."[84] Overall, the tower gave the relatively small H. C. Price Co. an identity in its townscape. As Joe Price recalled, "It gave the company its whole groundwork for the type of company it was. We had no problem being a company in a town with Phillips because the tower gave us our own pride, our own place."[85]

Conclusion: The Price Tower and Mid-Century Skyscrapers
The Price Tower was in some respects an anachronism when it was conceived and built in the 1950s. In that period, among American tall buildings, there was what in retrospect appears as a convergence toward a normative type of glass tower, rectangular in plan and minimally ornamented. Much architectural thought focused on such towers' proportions and the refinement of their details, especially the metal frames of their glass curtain walls. Prominent examples in the United States included Pietro Belluschi's Equitable Savings and Loan Association Building, Portland, Oregon (1944-48); Harrison and Abramowitz's United Nations Secretariat, New York (1947-50); Lever House, New York (1950-52), by Gordon Bunshaft for Skidmore, Owings and Merrill; and Ludwig Mies van der Rohe's Lake Shore Drive Apartments, Chicago (1949-51) and Seagram Building, New York (1954-58), the latter designed with Philip Johnson.[86] The overtly ornamental Price Tower appeared out of step as a variation on Sullivan's skyscrapers that had been Wright's introduction to the type in the 1890s. When the design was unveiled in 1953, *Architectural Forum* observed, "At first glance such a tower might seem anachronistic in an age that delights to honor such flat surface masterpieces as Lever House, an age when even the bosses stamped into the Alcoa Tower and the spider web on the UN Secretariat are called three-dimensional. Here is an office building that is all flowering ornament—ornament, in Wright's words, 'of the building, not on it.' Here is a tower whose surfaces have depth, whose form is manifestly intended to 'transcend function and be touched with poetic imagination.' And it is true that no thoroughbred business building has been so richly adorned since Wright's own 'Lieber Meister' Louis Sullivan laced the entire envelope of his [1896] Guaranty Building in Buffalo with terra cotta cast in delicate patterns (Fig. 2.19). But this 'anachronism' of ornament is studied, deliberate, and defiant. Is this then the last skyscraper of another age?"[87]

Wright was highly critical of the modernist convention of the glass box, especially in the case of the United Nations Secretariat. Among other notable skyscrapers

84 Bill Creel, interview with Sue Lacey and Arn Henderson, 21 August 1990, 6. PTAC Archives.

85 Joe Price, interview with Sue Lacey, 26 February 1990, 14. PTAC Archives.

86 On Belluschi's Equitable Building, see Meredith L. Clausen, **Pietro Belluschi: Modern American Architect** (Cambridge, Mass.: M.I.T. Press, 1994), 164-72. On the United Nations, see Victoria Newhouse, **Wallace K. Harrison, Architect** (New York: Rizzoli, 1989), 104-143. On Lever House, see Carol Krinsky, **Gordon Bunshaft of Skidmore, Owings and Merrill** (New York: Architectural History Foundation; and Cambridge, Mass.: MIT Press, 1988), 18-26. On Mies's post-war steel and glass towers, see William H. Jordy, **American Buildings and Their Architects, Volume 5: The Impact of European Modernism in the Mid-Twentieth Century** (New York: Oxford University Press, 1972), 221-77; Franz Schulze, **Mies van der Rohe: A Critical Biography** (Chicago: University of Chicago Press, 1986), 239-48, 270-83; and Phyllis Lambert, "Mies Immersion," in **Mies in America,** Phyllis Lambert, ed. (New York: Harry N. Abrams, 2001), 354-421. See also "High-Rise Office Buildings," **Progressive Architecture** 38 (June 1957): 159-91. Alfred Levitt with George G. Miller designed a type of eight-story apartment house in reinforced concrete with four apartments per floor and corner balconies, for the development of Levitt House (1958), in Beechhurst, Queens. See "Alfred Levitt, with New Ideas, Methods, Tackles Middle-Income Apartment Field," **Architectural Forum** 104 (February 1956): 16-17; "Apartment Colony Is Built on Principles of Light, Air and Space," **New York Times**, 24 February 1957; and Robert A.M. Stern, Thomas Mellins, and David Fishman, **New York 1960: Architecture and Urbanism between the Second World War and the Bicentennial** (New York: Monacelli, 1995), 1001-3.

87 "Frank Lloyd Wright's Concrete and Copper Skyscraper on the Prairie," 98.

Figure 2.20 Wallace Harrison and Max Abramowitz, Alcoa Building, Pittsburgh, Penn., completed 1953, featuring steel frame clad in aluminum exterior panels encompassing windows and stamped in a diamond pattern. Photograph courtesy of Alcoa.

that recently had been completed, the Price Tower might be superficially compared to Harrison and Abramowitz's Alcoa Building in Pittsburgh, opened in 1953 (Fig. 2.20). This thirty-story corporate symbol was the world's first aluminum-skinned skyscraper. Its system of diamond-patterned stamped panels incorporating windows was technically novel, and, like the Price Tower, the Alcoa Building embodied the period's ideal of innovation. The use of lightweight aluminum inside the building for pipes and ducts did enable the steel frame to be thirty to fifty per cent lighter than a conventional one. In this way, because of its technical novelty and quasi-ornamental metalwork, the Alcoa Tower represented the closest challenge to Wright's claims about the Price Tower's innovations as a lightweight construction with a consistent ornamental exterior. Yet the Alcoa Building's frame itself realized no original structural concept comparable to the Price Tower's. While at first glance the panels appear ornamental like Wright's copper panels for the Price Tower, the Alcoa Bower's cladding was affixed as an independent skin to its frame, whereas Wright took pains to see that the Price Tower's copper panels were cast with its concrete parapets.[88]

Wright said often that the idea of the modern skyscraper as a cage of steel was still conceptually like a box, wherein posts and beams constituted the frame. Thus while steel itself was a modern discovery, there had been no corresponding rethinking of its constructive use in tall buildings wherein its great tensile strength could be exploited to the fullest, as in the cantilevered tower. Harold Price, Jr., recalled that Wright was always making negative remarks about Mies, Le Corbusier, the Seagram Building, and Lever House in New York, as tall buildings that pushed people into a box. According to Wright, they were not consistent with human demands, whereas he claimed that he was "building from the inside out for his clients' needs."[89] As he said to the A.I.A. in 1954, "The old architecture has gone. You see, the old architecture was a box and the corners of that were the supports....the box form is now the old thinking and the old thought, and what you hear of as the International Style is, of course, the old box with its face lifted. You make the box walls of glass and you look into the box. Has the thought changed? Never! The same old thought; no real dissidence. That is not modern architecture, that is only contemporary. There is a distinction I wish you'd remember because it's a valid one and it's a genuine basic structural reason for what we call organic architecture."[90]

For Wright, his solution for the tall building embodied in the Price Tower was both technically advanced and materially economical, hence truly modern. It was also dramatic confirmation of his lifelong belief that architecture should imitate nature rather than historical or contemporary styles. This had been Sullivan's principle, and it had animated his early prototypical solutions for the tall office building of the 1890s that Wright had admired. For Wright, the idea that tied his work to Sullivan's was signified by the word 'plasticity.' As Wright often said, he wanted to take Sullivan's idea of plasticity in ornamentation of surfaces to another level by introducing it into the three-dimensional form of modern buildings. To Wright, this meant abandoning the idea of the frame as essential to conventional construction, from the log cabin to the modern office tower. Wright wrote of Sullivan, "If form

88 On the Alcoa Building, see Newhouse, **Wallace Harrison**, 145-49, and "Alcoa Complete," **Architectural Forum** 99 (November 1953): 124-31. Wright's critique of the United Nations Headquarters appeared in "We Must Shape True Inspiration," **New York Times Magazine**, 20 April 1957, in **Frank Lloyd Wright: Collected Writings**, volume 4 (1939-1949), ed. Bruce Brooks Pfeiffer (New York: Rizzoli, 1992), 305-6.

89 HCPJr., telephone conversation with author, 20 July 2004.

90 FLW, address to Detroit Chapter, American Institute of Architects, 27 May 1954, in **Truth Against the World: Frank Lloyd Wright Speaks for an Organic Architecture**, ed. Patrick J. Meehan, (New York: John Wiley & Sons, 1987), 320. At an exhibit of his work including the Price Tower model at the gallery of the National Institute of Arts and Letters and the American Academy of Arts and Letters, Wright said, "A box is more a coffin for the human spirit than an inspiration. The classic or camouflaged old post-and-lintel box in the glassed-in cage or the glass-walled dwelling. Old Man Box merely looks different when it's glassified, that's all." Wright, quoted in Aline B. Louchheim, "Wright Analyzes Architect's Need," **New York Times**, 26 May 1953, 23. The exhibition was at the institute's gallery on Audubon Terrace, off Broadway, between 155th and 156th streets. "Famed Architect to Get Medal of Arts Institute," **New York Times**, 14 May 1953, 10.

really followed function—it did by means of this ideal of plasticity—why not throw away the implications of post or upright and beam or horizontal entirely. Have no beams or columns piling up as 'joinery'… Now why not let walls, ceilings, floors become *seen* as component parts of each other, their surfaces flowing into each other to get continuity in the whole, eliminating all constructed features just as Louis Sullivan had eliminated background in his ornament in favor of an integral sense of the whole. Here an ideal began to have consequences."[91] In his towers Wright abandoned the steel frame, which Sullivan had retained. Yet Wright transferred the principle of plasticity that he saw in Sullivan's ornament to the continuity of the tower's reinforced concrete structure of piers and cantilevers. To Wright, the age-old box form sustained a traditional practice in the use of materials that did not explore modern steel's unique expressive possibilities, which he saw embodied in cantilever construction.

In this way, while the Price Tower with its ornamental detail superficially resembles works like the Guaranty, its structural continuity realized Wright's aim of embodying Sullivan's ideal of plasticity in three dimensions. Along the Guaranty's vertical piers, Sullivan's ornamental patterns in terra cotta strove to represent the vitality of the modern steel frame as a system of columns and beams that sustained large compressive and tensile stresses. In his view, a vital modern architecture should present the building as a living, natural form whose ornament conveyed its drama of load and support. Sullivan wrote of the pier, "Simple as it seems and is to our sense of sight, it is nevertheless compound; for it is the field of operation of the two synchronous forces—downward and upward… But the moment this lintel (this latent thing), is laid upon the two piers and connects their activities—presto! by the subtlest of conceivable magic, instantly the Science of Architecture comes into being."[92] In its structural system of piers and cantilevers, Wright's Price Tower on the prairie was an original experiment in the science of architecture. Wright sought to supersede Sullivan's duality of load and support with a continuity of structure based on the plasticity of steel-reinforced concrete.

In its vitality as constructed form, with loads artfully balanced on its concrete frame, the Price Tower was for Wright like a living organism. At different times, he invoked the metaphor of a tree or an upraised hand; Joe Price recurrently spoke of the building as like the human form.[93] Yet the Price Tower was so different in construction, both from Adler and Sullivan's towers and from glass boxes of the 1950s, that it does not fit conventional historiography of the type in the twentieth century. In our minds, next to the normative Seagram Building of the same years, the Price Tower looks like a different species of tall building, as Wright intended it to be. It was not another variation on the steel-framed box with a superficially novel cladding, like other postwar modernist towers. Rather the Price Tower was genuinely new in its structural and spatial plasticity. In this sense, Wright's tall building on the prairie was an extension of Sullivanian principles, but it was less "the last skyscraper of another age" than it was a model of what the type's future might be. ■ ■ ■

91 Frank Lloyd Wright, An Autobiography (1932), in Frank Lloyd Wright: Collected Writings, volume 2, 1930-1932, ed. Bruce Brooks Pfeiffer (New York: Rizzoli, 1992), 206.

92 Louis Sullivan, "Kindergarten Chat 37: The Elements of Architecture: Objective and Subjective, (1): Pier and Lintel," in Kindergarten Chats and Other Writings, ed. Isabella Athey (1947; New York: Dover, 1979), 121-22.

93 Joe Price said, "And if you notice the Tower as you walk around it, one of the most beautiful things is to drive around it and watch the personality change as you're moving around the building. There's a completely different building from just 10 ft. It'll totally change, it is like a human being. When you walk around them they change from different angles, and they are hard to recognize from one side or the other. The tower is this way." Joe Price, interview with Sue Lacey, 26 February 1990, 23. PTAC Archives.

INTERIORS, FURNITURE, AND FURNISHINGS

Pat Kirkham and Scott W. Perkins

"Trifles make perfection but perfection is no trifle."[1]

Evidence of Frank Lloyd Wright's perfectionism and pleasure in detail and form is everywhere apparent in the interiors and furnishings of the Price Tower, as is his ability to achieve unity of effect between interior and exterior as well as within buildings conceived as total works of art. Drawing on contemporary sources, including extant objects, this chapter focuses on the interiors, furniture, and furnishings as they were in the mid-1950s when the building was opened. It concludes with responses to and recollections of them by people who lived and worked in the Price Tower.

Context

Skyscrapers were by no means new by 1956, but high-rise offices and apartments remained major markers of modernity. The Price Tower interiors should be seen within the wider framework of an increasing acceptance in postwar America of "modern" form in all areas of design, from magazine graphics and movie advertising to furniture, interiors, and architecture. The commissioning of the Price Tower coincided with the post-World War II boom in corporate architecture and interior design, and an increasing concern for work environments that were pleasant to inhabit and increased productivity. Much of what was being built for corporate America, however, related more to the steel frames and glass curtain walls of International Style Modernism than to the quirky, richly-patterned and, at times, Arts and Crafts-like modernity of Wright at the Price Tower. Had Harold, Jr., and Joe Price advised their father to consult with one of the architectural firms that specialized in expressing the "modern" approach to business of companies such as Alcoa, IBM, and CBS through sleek, rectilinear, high-rise office blocks, the results would have been dramatically different.[2]

The commissioning of the Price Tower also coincided with a revival of interest in decoration, in many cases by architects and designers strongly influenced by International Style Modernism, a movement associated with the eschewal of decoration. From the inter-war years, Wright's consistent embrace of the decorative within discourses of rationality, utility, and machine production had stood as an example of an alternative modernity to that of the Modern Movement (labeled the International Style in the early 1930s), but he died before it became clear just how important this revival of interest in the decorative would be. Wright, of course, was only one of many influences on the interior design of younger designers such as Charles and Ray Eames and Alexander Girard,[3] but the connection serves as a reminder that the interiors of the Price Tower were designed at a pivotal moment in American design when attitudes towards "the decorative" within the modern were being re-assessed.

Unity of Effect and *Gesamtkunstwerk*

Few architects had Wright's ability to achieve harmony and unity of effect within particular rooms, let alone between rooms and between inside and out. Wright ranks alongside other "greats" such as Robert Adam, Josef Hoffman, and Charles Rennie and Margaret Macdonald Mackintosh, in his imaginative interconnecting and cross referencing of parts within a unified whole. Like them, Wright was a great maker of pattern[4] as well as a designer capable of seemingly endless variations on a motif or visual theme. The Price Tower is an excellent example of *Gesamtkunstwerk*, a concept popular in late nineteenth and early twentieth cen-

FOOTNOTES

As a matter of consistency, we have used William Allin Storrer, **The Frank Lloyd Wright Companion** (Chicago: University of Chicago Press, 1993) as the source for dating Wright's projects.

1 Frank Lloyd Wright to Harold C. Price, Sr. (subsequently referred to as FLW and HCPSr, respectively), letter, 28 December 1955. Archives of the History of Art, The Getty Center for Art and the Humanities, Los Angeles. FLWA.

2 At the Connecticut General building in Bloomfield, Connecticut, a building contemporaneous with the Price Tower (it opened in 1957), for example, architect Gordon Bunshaft of SOM (Skidmore Owings & Merrill) contained open-plan flexible office spaces within sheer glass walls. Although the two buildings were outwardly very different, there were some similarities between this project and the Price Tower, not least their close relationship to open countryside. Frazar Wilder, President of Connecticut General, believed so strongly in pleasant work environments that he relocated the company from Hartford to a 280 acre farm in rural Connecticut. There was no urban landscape surrounding the building as at the Price Tower, but the Connecticut General headquarters indicate that Wright was not alone at mid-century in envisaging offices with direct views of open countryside.

3 See Pat Kirkham, **Charles and Ray Eames: Designers of the Twentieth Century**, (Cambridge, Mass.: MIT Press, 1995), 143-199 and **The Opulent Eye of Alexander Girard**, brochure published by the Cooper-

Figure 3.1   View of Harold C. Price's Office on the 19th Floor, 1955-1956. Photograph by Steven Brooke Studios, 2004.

tury Europe and America that regarded interiors and everything therein as a "total work of art." Wright was not the first architect to apply the concept to non-domestic interiors but his Larkin Building (Buffalo, NY, 1903) was an influential application of such principles to office space. It was not until the Price Tower, however, that Wright had an opportunity to see realized his designs for integrated office and domestic interiors. Only at the Price Tower did multivalent interconnections operate *between* as well as *within* domestic and non-domestic spaces.

The interrelationships of the interiors and their parts at the Price Tower epitomize what Wright called "the integrity of each in all and all in each" within an organic whole that was the building in its entirety.[5] Discussing the Price Tower, Wright's former apprentice and son-in-law, William Wesley Peters, stated "Mr. Wright was always willing to design…a lot of appurtenances in the interior design because then that made it all one organic whole…Mr. Wright always believed, along with Louis Sullivan, his master, that you should perceive the design of the building from general to particulars…This he really strove to do in every building…The Price Tower went pretty far along that [way of] thinking."[6]

The holistic unity of the interiors results, to a large degree, from complementarity of form and motif and, as in much good pattern-making, there is a strong underlying order. Wright likened internal disorder in architecture and design to a disease (one he feared was nearly fatal[7]) and, for most of his career, used modular schemes based on geometric form to ensure order in his work. Although not unusual in his work across the years, there was a strong emphasis on the geometric in commissions of the 1950s, including a commission undertaken shortly before the Price Tower, namely the William and Mary Palmer House, Ann Arbor, Michigan (1950). There, equilateral triangles and the hexagons they formed when multiplied were the dominant modules.[8] At the Price Tower, Wright used a favorite 30-60-90° triangle, doubled it to form an equilateral triangle, and then doubled that to form an equilateral parallelogram—the modular unit for the interior floor plans (all the walls and partitions fall on unit lines or subdivisions thereof).[9] The dialectic between triangles and parallelograms, between each of those and hexagons, and between the modular and the "one-off," as well as the weaving of non-geometric pattern through all the rooms, ensured that the interiors never felt or looked "modular." Grant Hildebrand described the Palmer House interiors as a "beautifully crafted encapsulation of a half century of Wright's pattern"; the same could be said of the Price Tower interiors.[10]

Interplay of Parts

Permutations of repeating, complementary, and contrasting forms, motifs, materials, and colors accounted for much of the visual stimulation of the Price Tower interiors as well as the cohesion; just when one thinks one has explored every modulation and rhythm, another layer unfolds. There is considerable repetition. For example, the scrolling "bean sprout" pattern on the copper edging of the bookcases, mural frame, and lampshade in Harold Price's office was repeated elsewhere in the building, including the fireplace in the rented apartments (Figs. 3.1–3.2). Not all the complementary links were as subtle as Wright's use of the "bean sprout" inner motif of this pattern to form the inner curve of the aluminum handrails (Fig. 3.3). More often, complementarity involved Wright reconfiguring a motif within a broad repeat of a shape, as in the case of the large square ceiling lights that complement the square bronze company logos (designed by Wright) cast into the center point of the floors of the elevator lobby (Fig. 3.4). Sometimes the scale remained

Hewitt, National Design Museum, Smithsonian Institution, in conjunction with the eponymous exhibition, September 2000 to March 2001. The work of the Eameses and Girard can be categorized as proto-'post modern' and it is perhaps no coincidence that Bruce Goff, the great admirer of Wright who suggested Wright for the Price Tower, would go on to create some of the most idiosyncratic 'post-modern' interiors in the USA.

4 Grant Hildebrand, **The Wright Space: Pattern and Meaning in Frank Lloyd Wright's Houses** (Seattle: University of Washington Press, 1991), 18-27.

5 Frank Lloyd Wright, "To the Young Man in Architecture," in **Frank Lloyd Wright Collected Writings**, vol. 2, 1930-1932, ed. Bruce Brooks Pfeiffer (New York: Rizzoli, 1992), 92.

6 William Wesley Peters, interview with Sue Lacey, 27 February 1990, 12-13. Price Tower Arts Center (subsequently referred to as PTAC) Archives.

7 Wright, "To the Young Man in Architecture," 92.

8 For Palmer Residence see Hildebrand, **The Wright Space**, 142-145.

9 Peters, interview with Sue Lacey, 27 February 1990, 16. PTAC Archives. For Wright's geometric grids and the Price Tower see Storrer, **The Wright Companion**, 378-379.

10 Hildebrand, **The Wright Space**, 142.

Figure 3.2 Detail of Copper Edging, ca. 1955. Harold Price's Office, 19th Floor. The equilateral triangles and half-hexagons in this decorative edging were both elements in Wright's basic parallelogram module for the building. The copper edging is repeated throughout the interiors and form a link between them. The central "bean sprout" element can be seen at the final curl of the aluminum handrail in Fig. 3.3. Photograph by Steven Brooke Studios, 2004.

Figure 3.3 Aluminum Stairway Handrail, ca. 1955. Used outside and inside the building, the handrail was made by curling a flat strip of aluminum. Wright gave the inner curved edge of the rail the same hook-like form as that on the "bean sprout" motif in the copper edging seen in Fig. 3.2. Photograph by Steven Brooke Studios, 2004.

Figure 3.4 Elevator Lobby, 1955. The vertical axis of the Tower is the elevator lobby located on every floor. The ceiling light fixture complements the brass floor logo medallion embedded in the pigmented concrete floor. This view shows a drinking fountain (left), and offers a glimpse into a furnished office space, and illustrates the angularity of the architecture and its lowered ceiling height. Photograph by Joe Price (PTAC 2003.16.285).

Figure 3.5   Office Desk, designed ca. 1955. (Catalogue No. 42) (PTAC 2001.01.080). The elongated hexagonal Philippine mahogany desk, typical of the Tower's offices, featured triangular drawer fronts and pulls, aluminum half-round trim, and hidden storage for an angular waste can. The desk appears to float upon narrow planes of wood capped in enameled copper. Photograph by Steven Brooke Studios, 2004.

the same, sometimes not. For example, differences in size and materials made the use of the logo on office doors and china both repetitive and complementary.

A consistent color palette also helped integrate the different aspects of a building that included both offices and apartments. Light tones (walls and ceilings) were offset by brown (Philippine mahogany, golden-tinted glass, and copper), "Cherokee Red," one of Wright's favorite colors[11] (floors, metal bases of desks, and markings on windows and chairs), pinky-rose/red (polished copper and upholstery fabric), green/turquoise (patinated copper), "silver" (aluminum edgings, painted chairs, and mirror glass), and the odd touch of blue. Throughout the building the shine of the floor reflected the shine of polished copper, glass, mirror glass, and aluminum. Such rich overtones offset the workaday practicality of interiors that also spelled out their modernity through state-of-the-art elevators, forced air heating, and air conditioning.

Wright's appreciation of nature is well known,[12] but at the Price Tower natural materials and colors evocative of nature were used alongside those that evoked machine mass-production. Flagging both the modernity of the building and its links with nature, Wright used them to create sophisticated urban interiors. He also used similar but subtly different mixes of materials in different rooms; for example, the materials for the furniture and fittings in the "typical office" were mahogany and aluminum and in the "typical apartment" mahogany, aluminum, and copper, while in Harold Price's office they were mahogany, copper, and mirror glass. In the case of the four types of aluminum chairs designed for the building, the permutations of the individual elements were such that any of the types could be placed in a room without disrupting the harmony therein. Contrasts—between

11 Peters, interview with Sue Lacey, 27 February 1990, 17. PTAC Archives.

12 Frank Lloyd Wright, **The Natural House** (New York: Horizon, 1954), 49-62.

13 Peters, interview with Sue Lacey, 27 February 1990, 3. PTAC Archives.

14 See Frank Lloyd Wright, **An Autobiography** (New York: Horizon, 1943), 142, as quoted in Hildebrand, **The Wright Space**, 27.

15 "H.C. Price Company Had Humble Beginning," **The Bartlesville Examiner**, 9 February 1956.

16 These are very different than the "glass box" high rise offices and apartments with floor-to-ceiling glass walls and more or less unimpeded consumption of "views" we are familiar with today.

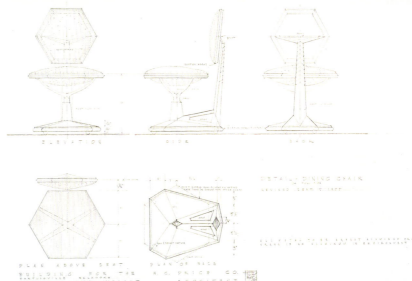

Figure 3.6 Commissary Tables and Stools, designed 1956. (Catalogue Nos. 52, 53, 54) (PTAC 2001.01.016, 2001.01.025, 2001.01.28). The commissary's patinated copper furniture included triangular tables and hexagonal stools topped with colorful cushions. The edge detail of the tables and chairs complemented that of Harold Price's office furnishings, while the patinated surface complemented the Tower's exterior copper panels and fins. Photograph by Steven Brooke Studios, 2004.

Figure 3.7 Drawing, Aluminum Dining Chair, 1955. Wright's aluminum furniture designs included this dining chair, used by the Prices in their apartment. The hexagon seat cushion sits like a jewel in a setting, atop a multi-faceted base of cast aluminum. A "casual" chair version, with arms, is shown in Fig. 3.18. Both chairs have fixed seats and backs, and were originally upholstered in Wright's "Taliesin" fabrics for Schumacher. FLWF 5215.209. © Frank Lloyd Wright Foundation.

small, near-claustrophobic, spaces (elevators and entryways to the apartments[13]) and larger more expansive ones (double-height living rooms and lobbies), materials (especially wood and metal), and overtly "modern" designs as opposed to ones that drew heavily on the Arts and Crafts Movement of the late nineteenth and early twentieth century—drew attention to difference and dramatized particular features.

Indoors and Out

The mediation between indoors and out was central to Wright's approach to design. He sought to destroy "the box" by opening up walls and providing vistas between rooms and between indoor spaces and the outdoors by means of broad horizontal windows that flooded rooms with natural light.[14] The *Bartlesville Morning Examiner* noted that "every unit [was] an outside unit"[15] but Wright saw terraces as *intermediaries* between an interior and the "nature" beyond. The stunning views of the Oklahoma countryside were also mediated through sun-louver "fins," tinted glass, and window frames (some emphasized by painted struts and accents). Such features broke up and "framed" the panoramas while serving as reminders of enclosure—of the very fact of being *inside* a building.[16]

Furniture

Wright designed all the built-in furniture at the Price Tower as well as some freestanding pieces for offices, apartments, and the commissary. The Phillipine mahogany furniture fused unusual forms with more or less conventional furniture types (e.g., desk, table, stool, book case) often to quite dramatic effect (Fig. 3.5), as did the more idiosyncratic metal furniture. Copper, rarely the main material for furniture in modern times, was used by Wright in patinated form for stunning indoor/outdoor furniture designed for the commissary (see below and Fig. 3.6; also Catalogue Nos. 52, 53, 54). In contrast to this ancient material, he specified aluminum, a relatively new material, for a series of upholstered chairs with hexagonal seats and backs, vertical "spines," and faceted bases (Fig 3.7).[17] Of all the objects in the Tower, these anthropomorphic chairs, likened to humanoids, robots, and barbers' chairs and described as "futuristic" and "space-age," mark the interiors they inhabit as "ultra-modern."[18]

Metal furniture based on primary forms was not new to Wright;[19] he had used geometric form in furniture for the Larkin Building (1903) and the S.C. Johnson & Son Wax Building (Racine, WI, 1936) where he also provided office seating to meet the

17 John Calvin Womack, **A Report on Floors 17, 18, and 19, Price Tower, Bartlesville, Oklahoma, Frank Lloyd Wright Architect**, (National Endowment for the Arts Grant Report #0342006019, 2004), 39. Few of the original chairs remain. Some have rubber bumpers, added to prevent the metal from damaging the wooden desks and scuffing the shoes of those sitting in them. Painted accents, in red, are found on the bases and vertical supports of some chairs, but whether or not this was specified by Wright is not known.

18 Photographs of these chairs were shown to three groups of students at the Bard Graduate Center for Studies in the Decorative Arts, Design, and Culture in November 2005. These were the most common comments made.

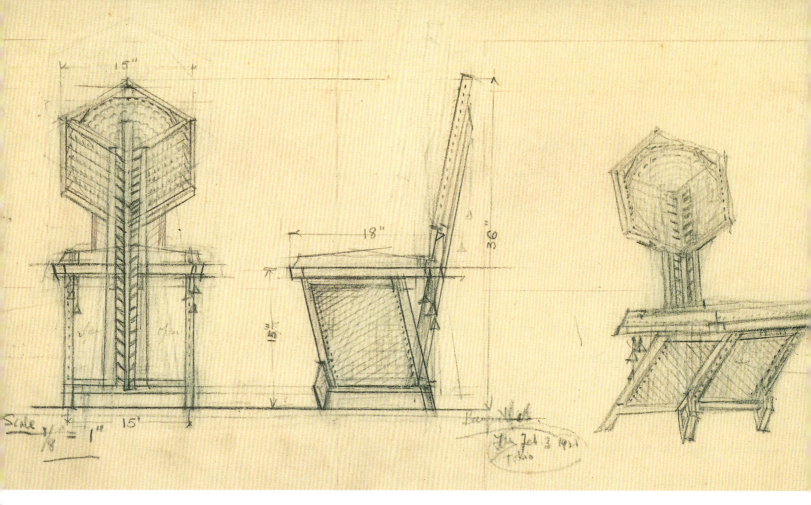

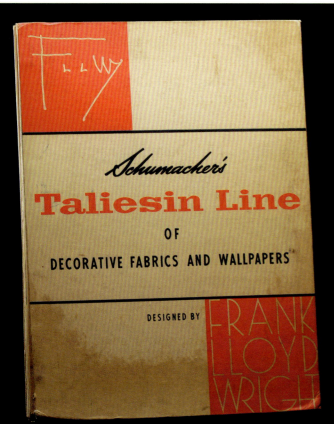

Figure 3.8   Dining Chair, Imperial Hotel, Tokyo. (Catalogue No. 5). The Imperial Hotel's "Peacock" chair (designed 1916) combined rectilinear and hexagonal forms. Its spine, though made of wood, is similar to the cast aluminum spine of the Price Tower dining and casual chairs. FLWF 1509.057. © Frank Lloyd Wright Foundation

Figure 3.9   Schumacher's Taliesin Line of Decorative Fabrics and Wallpapers designed by Frank Lloyd Wright, 1955. (Catalogue No. 64) (PTAC 2005.01). Photograph by Amatucci Photography, 2004.

19 See Anthony Alofsin, **Frank Lloyd Wright: The Lost Years, 1910-1922** (Chicago: University of Chicago, 1993), 153-220.

20 See Edgar Kaufmann, Jr., "Frank Lloyd Wright's Architecture Exhibited," **Metropolitan Museum of Art Bulletin** (Fall 1982): 38.

21 FLWF 5215.07

Figure 3.10 Schumacher's Taliesin Line of Decorative Fabrics and Wallpapers designed by Frank Lloyd Wright, 1955. (Catalogue No. 64) (PTAC 2005.01). Detail of Taliesin design #501 with sample #734632 (Brick color) and #734623 (Granite color) specified for bedspread, bedroom draperies, and chairs in the Price family apartment and for chairs in the Price Company offices. Photograph by Amatucci Photography, 2004.

needs of different users. Hexagonal backed chairs, in wood rather than metal, were designed for the Imperial Hotel, Tokyo (1916–22, Fig. 3.8).[20] Wright's early design for the Price Tower "typical apartment" included wood seat furniture[21] but he decided upon aluminum for the dining chairs as well as for those used in the offices. Aluminum signified "modernity" but, despite the efforts of designers such as Marcel Breuer, Gio Ponti, and Warren McArthur in the 1930s, it had never taken off as a material for furniture, largely because it proved too expensive, brittle, and inflexible.[22] World War II transformed the aluminum industry, increasing its production capacity by 600 per cent, and after the war new non-military uses were sought for what manufacturers claimed as a "new" wonder material with enormous potential for mass production. Wright was one of the first major designers to respond to the challenge of designing furniture in aluminum in the 1950s but, partly because of this, it proved difficult to transform his designs into objects and there was considerable hand production involved in those used at the Price Tower.[23]

By using such an exotic material, Wright was able to stamp the Price Tower interiors as boldly "modern," but it proved nearly impossible to find a manufacturer for his designs. Indeed, he complained to Harold Price that the aluminum chairs had caused him more headaches than the entire building.[24] The chairs were eventually made in Oklahoma, at the Blue Stem Foundry in nearby Dewey, using a "low-tech" sand-casting technique.[25] Despite extensive buffing, the surfaces remained discolored and somewhat rough, and the frames were painted a "bright aluminum color" in order to cover the imperfections.[26] These chairs have nothing of the smooth, sleek finish of the Eames Aluminum Chairs (1958) that were also produced by a sand-casting process but one developed over a considerable period of time by the Herman Miller Furniture Company and the Eames Office.[27] The upholstery was undertaken by Bell's Auto Upholstery, Bartlesville, using fabrics from Wright's 1955 textile collection for F. Schumacher & Company, New York, one of the leading textile companies of the period. (Figs. 3.9, 3.10) For the most part, Wright created unique designs for the Price Tower, but in some of the interiors discussed below other fabrics he designed for Schumacher, as well as furniture from a mass production range for the Heritage-Henredon Furniture Company (1955), were used.

Main Entrance and Lobby
The ceiling and lights of the entrance lobby remain the first place that visitors encounter a distinctive disposition of planes (based on triagonal or "flattened pyramid" forms) that are repeated throughout the building (Fig 3.11). Here the patinated copper frames offset white opaque glass; similar frames elsewhere in the building remain unpatinated. In the lobby (Figs. 1.20 & 3.12), the "Cherokee" red floor added a touch of the vernacular to this soaring space, the modernity of which was defined by the double-height ceiling, pale walls, natural and electric light, and geometric form. The gallery, reminiscent of those in Arts and Crafts interiors, added medieval overtones as did the hassock-style seating and "fluted" walls, reminiscent of medieval choir stalls and linen-fold paneling, respectively. The sparseness of the "fluting," the hexagonal form, and cantilever structure of the seats were among the more obvious markers of modernity in Wright's rich mix of modern and pre modern imagery.

22 Christopher Wilk, **Marcel Breuer: Furniture and Interiors** (New York: Museum of Modern Art, 1990), 116-118 and Sarah Nichols ed., **Aluminum by Design** (Pittsburgh: Carnegie Museum of Art, 2000), 44-51.

23 Kirkham, **Eames**, 246 citing Dennis Doorman, "Designing an Aluminum World: Industrial Designers and the American Aluminum Industry." Paper presented at "Industry and Anti-industry" organized by the International Design History Society at the Victoria & Albert Museum, London, December 1990. For Eames Office work in aluminum see Kirkham, **Eames**, 246-254.

24 FLW to HCPSr, letter, 28 December 1955. Archives of the History of Art, The Getty Center for Art and the Humanities, Los Angeles. FLWA.

25 Cecil Magana, in discussion with Kirkham and Perkins, Bartlesville, October 2004.

26 Ibid. Wright made reference to the finish on FLWF 5215.210.

27 Kirkham, **Eames**, 246-248.

Figure 3.11 Ceiling and Lighting, Entry Lobby, 1955. Visitors first experience the complexity of the Tower's architecture in the Entry Lobby, where multiple angles, double-height ceiling, and light-colored walls are markers of its modernity. Triangular ceiling lights framed in copper introduce a design form and material used throughout the building's interiors. Photograph by Joe Price (PTAC 2003.16.132).

Despite the gallery, the dominant emphasis is vertical; our eyes are lifted upward to the "star"-studded ceiling of simple triangular lights, just as our minds are lifted to loftier purpose by the painted inscription (Fig.3.13). Harold Price wanted a mural in the lobby. Wright did not, although he often incorporated them into buildings.[28] When Price complained that inadequate supervision meant that certain things had not been followed through, including the mural, Wright shot back testily, "There is to be no mural in the entrance if I can help it, as I have told everybody who mentioned it to me—including you. I like the dignity of the beautiful wall left alone."[29] The text on the west wall probably represents a compromise between client and architect. Wright edited and adapted Walt Whitman to suit his own purposes and the quotations not only reinforce an Arts and Crafts ambiance but also serve to introduce the 89-year-old architect: "I make the signal to remain after me in sight forever."[30]

In the entrance lobby one could buy newspapers and cigars from an area fitted out by Wright or consult the directory board to ascertain which tenants occupied which floors.[31] One the four hexagonal elevators tucked away at the rear of the lobby was reserved for residents, the others for commercial traffic. Wright did not believe in wasting space on elevators, stairwells, or lobbies and each elevator was only approximately ten square feet each. He did believe in designing them specifically for the building they were to service, however, and the unusual shape of these meant that they had to be specially manufactured.[32]

Offices

Two extant Wright drawings for a "typical office"[33] show desks with elongated hexagonal tops set at a 30° angle to the exterior wall, as in a 1956 photograph that also shows the 5/8-inch half-round aluminum molding that trimmed the desks, full-height glass partitions, and wall-mounted bookcases, making visual links to the aluminum chairs therein (Figs. 3.14, 3.15). The photograph also shows a small sitting area with upholstered settee and triangular-topped mahogany table. Copper end panels adorn the desks in the drawing, but this link to other interior and exterior panels was dropped from the final design that retained the hexagonal-shaped top, the angles of which were echoed in shallow triangular drawer fronts with triangular brass pulls (Fig. 3.16). The desktop form reappeared on the built-in dining tables, some of which, in later years, were used as desks when most of the apartments were converted to offices.

A drawing of Harold Price's penthouse office on the nineteenth floor (Fig. 3.17)[34] emphasized light and access to a terrace as well as the interplay between the vertical and the horizontal. As realized, however, there is a distinct air of cozy comfortableness in this retreat cum workspace (Fig. 3.18). Warm natural colors were amplified by the warm copper color, including that on a wood-burning fireplace that exuded literal and metaphorical warmth. The fireplace referenced domesticity, as did a copper pendant light, the shade of which was in a style that had graced Arts and Crafts interiors half a century earlier (Fig. 3.19). Adding to the domestic ambiance of the area between the fireplace and Price's workspace was a low banquette, one edge of which slid under the double-sided "partner's desk," offering the company president the chance to catnap during working hours. The view from one side of the desk was the terrace on which stood a "pretty good sized tree."[35] Much larger than the tiny terraces in the apartments, this was the only office in the building to have an outdoor space and the only terrace spacious enough to sit out and enjoy the view. In the other direction were

28 For examples of residential mural painting by Wright and others see Paul Kruty, "Art for Architecture: Mural Painting in the Prairie School," **Block Points** Vol. 3 (1998), 8-31.

29 HCPSr to FLW, letter, 27 December 1955, and FLW to HCPSr, letter, 28 December 1955. Archives of the History of Art, The Getty Center for Art and the Humanities, Los Angeles. FLWA.

30 Peters, interview with Sue Lacey, 27 February 1990, 9. PTAC Archives.

31 For Wright's design for a directory board see FLWF 5215.175. It remains in the Price Tower Arts Center's collection. PTAC 2001.01.103.

32 They required special opening mechanisms and were made by the Otis Elevator Company.

33 FLWF 5215.187A and FLWF 5215.009.

34 FLWF 5215.008.

35 Peters, interview with Sue Lacey, 27 February 1990, 21. PTAC Archives.

Figure 3.12   Ceiling and Wall Fluting, Entry Lobby, 1955. The "star"-studded ceiling and full-height triangular "fluting" in the Entry Lobby are complemented by the angularity of the gallery (seen from below). Aluminum door and window trim, ventilation grills, and the translucent triangular light covers are also visible. Photograph by Joe Price (PTAC 2003.16.257).

PENTHOUSE OFFICE OF MR. PRICE

Figure 3.17 Drawing, "Penthouse Office of Mr. Price," 1952. (Catalogue No. 28). Wright's early perspective drawing of Harold Price's office illustrates the dramatic ceiling height, large expanse of windows, and scored concrete floor. It does not show the cast aluminum seating or glass mirror wall mural. FLWF 5215.017. © Frank Lloyd Wright Foundation.

Figure 3.18 Harold Price's Office on the 19th Floor, 1956. Harold Price's office offered him a comfortable retreat atop the Price Tower. The mahogany desk and cabinetry are edged with copper trim, as is the Arts and Crafts-inspired pendant lamp and wood-burning fireplace that adds a touch of domesticity to the space. Three of the four aluminum casual chairs upholstered in red fabric that stood against the wall housing the mirror glass mural can be seen in this photograph. These modernity monikers contemporize the interior. Photograph by Joe Price (PTAC 2004.13).

Figure 3.19   Harold Price's Office on the 19th Floor, Showing Copper Fireplace, Pendant Lamp, and Desk, 1955-1956. The pendant lamp is the only hanging light fixture in the building. It suspends above Price's work surface, and is perhaps the object most reminiscent of Wright's domestic Prairie Style interiors. The open copper fireplace also adds to the Arts and Crafts ambience of this section of the office. The original draperies and carpet are shown in Fig. 3.18. Photograph by Steven Brooke Studios, 2004.

Figure 3.20   Detail, Wall Mural, Harold Price's Office, designed 1955. Designed by Wright in conjunction with Taliesin apprentice Eugene Masselink, the subtle colors of the layered mirror and painted glass wall mural reinforce the general palette of the room scheme. Often said to have been inspired by oil pipelines (an homage to the Price Company's business), the geometric forms of the "first abstract art in Bartlesville" are more representational of the building's triangular language. Photograph by Steven Brooke Studios, 2004.

The Commissary

The commissary was located on the sixteenth floor. Utilizing three of the floor's quadrants, it housed a small kitchen, dining rooms, and three open outdoor terraces offering panoramic views of Bartlesville and a worm's eye view of the copper spire housing the radio antennae. It was for this space that Wright designed a set of light, elegant furniture—twenty tables and forty chairs—made from pressed and patinated copper (see earlier Fig. 3.6) that coordinated with the interior and exterior copper panels as well as the tall copper louvers attached to the building. On the terrace of the commissary, the louvers could (and still can) be adjusted by hand for better control over protection from the wind and sun. The tops of the tables were trapezoidal while the tops of the stools were in the more familiar hexagon shape but all were edged with the familiar "bean sprout" trim while the bases, seemingly standing upon tiptoe, look as if they were modeled out of origami-style folded paper.[40] Meals were served on white china decorated with a red "HCP Co." logo (Fig. 3.22 and also see Catalogue No. 57) and manufactured by Shenango, a Pennsylvania-based firm specializing in restaurant ware. Peters recalls Wright designing "a lot of things" for this area, including "special trays for coffee services" but none are known to have survived.[41] The commissary offered the perk of free sandwiches and light entrees. "It was one of the neatest things," recalled a former secretary. "That was definitely one place where everybody got together... You never knew if you were going to have cold cuts or a full meal. They made chicken sometimes and spaghetti. As secretaries, especially, we'd just fly up there, woof down our lunch and then fly somewhere else."[42]

40 See **Frank Lloyd Wright: Seat of Genius** ed. Timothy A. Eaton (West Palm Beach: Eaton Fine Art, 1997), p. 58-61 for drawings and photographs of Wright's origami-like chairs for Taliesin and Florida Southern College.

41 Peters, interview with Sue Lacey, 27 February 1990,12. PTAC Archives.

42 Michelle (Schofner) Thompson, interview by Sue Lacey, 25 August 1990. PTAC Archives.

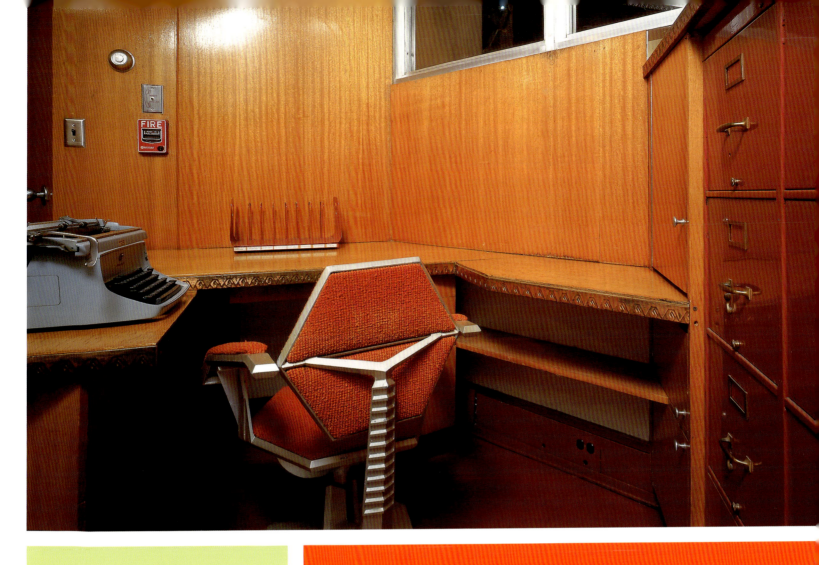

Figure 3.22 Dinner Plate with Price Company Logo, Shenango China Company, 1956 (Catalogue No. 57). The dinnerware used in the commissary was simple, white restaurant ware manufactured by the Shenango China Company, New Castle, PA, in 1956. The line featured a logo designed by Wright based upon that of the brass floor medallions in the elevator lobbies and used on glass doors throughout the Price Company offices. PTAC 2002.18.1-2. Photograph by Steven Brooke Studios, 2004.

was expected. Peter Wolcott ran the KVCW radio station from their living area, thus combining work and living on an even more intimate scale than Wright envisaged. Bruce Goff, the architect responsible for suggesting Wright to Price, so admired the building he had followed from inception to completion that he chose to live there from 1956 until 1963 (when he moved to Kansas City), albeit with the advantage of a reduced rent because of his close relationship with the Price family (Fig. 3.34).

Renting these high quality apartments proved a nearly impossible task in Bartlesville, and older residents with whom we discussed this matter were of the opinion that the rental costs ($285 per month) were thought to be too high for what was offered, given that such a sum covered a mortgage on a suburban family home.[63] There was no "culture of apartment living" in Bartlesville, as Mary Lou Price pointed out, and the apartments' idiosyncratic size and uniformity probably also worked to put off local renters.[64] Yet, despite finding the living space somewhat restrictive, the Wolcotts found their seventh and eighth floor apartment "extremely lovely."[65] Erna Wolcott-Conatser still speaks fondly of the building, and, in an interview given in 1990, recalled how wonderful it was as part of a young couple starting up life together to move to an apartment that was nicely carpeted and so much of the furniture fitted or provided that they only had to buy "the bed, utensils, pots and pans, and dishes."[66] They brought a television but, unlike the Price family apartment where the bookcases were altered to accommodate a television, kept it in their bedroom. Also unlike the Prices, they did not remodel the bedroom level because they needed the small bedroom for their child. Wolcott-Conatser's comments about the bedrooms, kitchen, and balcony can be summarized as "very, very small" and "very, very nice."[67]

It is all too easy to judge the kitchen by the standards of today, but even by US standards in the 1950s and 1960s the Price Tower kitchens were extremely small. Wolcott-Conatser, however, saw this as a positive feature of the kitchen she regarded as a marvel of modern technology. She stated, "You could stand in the middle...and you'd just work from there. It had everything...garbage disposal... refrigerator...stove...it was the most convenient kitchen ever, and you know, for its time that was very very unusual...many times I had Mr. and Mrs. Price [Harold Junior and Carolyn] over for dinner, prepared in a small kitchen."[68]

63 The Cage and the Tree, Educational Broadcasting Corporation in conjunction with New York University and WNET.

64 Peters, interview with Sue Lacey, 27 February 1990, 2. PTAC Archives.

65 Wolcott-Conaster, interview with Sue Lacey and Arn Henrderson, 22 August 1990, 4. PTAC Archives.

66 Ibid.

67 Ibid.

68 Ibid.

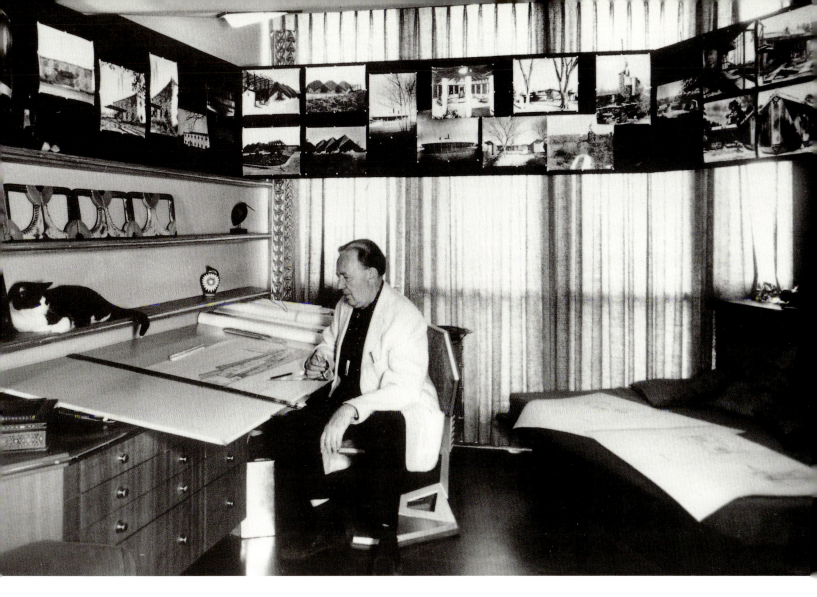

Figure 3.34 Bruce Goff with his cat, Chiaroscuro, in his office in the Price Tower, Bartlesville, Oklahoma, 1962. Bruce Goff, the person responsible for introducing Wright to Harold Price, occupied an apartment on floors 9 and 10 from 1956-1963—much of that time as the building's only residential tenant. This photograph of his architectural studio located on the bedroom level, offers an insight into how the space could be adapted for a variety of uses. Goff removed the top of the writing desk/bureau unit and replaced it with a drafting table. A "frieze" of photographs of his work banded the room, but maintained visual access to the living area below, and entry onto the terrace. He sits upon an aluminum dining chair. Doug Harris, photographer. Bruce A. Goff Archive, Ryerson and Burnham Archives, The Art Institute of Chicago.

She recalled most things positively, including the ways the upstairs shutters opened out to allow a view of the living room below, the triangular decorative patterns, and the Wright-designed furniture (dining table, chairs, hassocks). It is difficult to tell how far rose-tinted nostalgia has tempered her recall of leaking windows and ongoing problems with air conditioning and heating (there was not enough of either), but she did not dwell on such things, emphasizing rather the beauty of the building inside and out, landscaping kept "just perfect" by a full-time crew and the wonderful views. She compared the experience of living there to "being in New York in an elegant hotel," especially at night when one could see the lights of the city. What greater allusion to modern high-rise buildings could there be?

Goff and the Wolcotts, who moved from outside Bartlesville and shared a more modern outlook on life than many inhabitants of their newly adopted city, fall into that large category of clients who left Wright-designed homes reluctantly, minimized failings such as leaking windows or inadequate storage, and remembered them fondly as special places in which to live.[69] Their appreciation of the Price Tower interiors is testimony to Wright's ability to work wonders with small quarters and to create memorable living spaces. The Price Tower was and remains a special place—one easier to work in today with central air conditioning and heating, but alas, there are no apartments to rent… ■ ■ ■

69 Robert Twombly, Frank Lloyd Wright, His Life and His Architecture (New York: Wiley, 1979, 260), as quoted in Hildebrand, **The Wright Space**, 15.

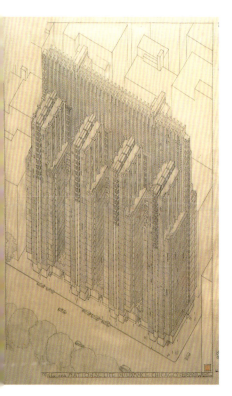

Figure 4.2   Axonometric view of the National Life Insurance Company Building, Chicago, project, 1924. FLWF 2404.001. © Frank Lloyd Wright Foundation.

In 1927, inspired by New York's booming real estate market, he asked Frank Lloyd Wright, a friend of more than twenty years, to design an apartment building on church property. Guthrie's aim was to generate rental income for the church and to repopulate the neighborhood with artsy, Greenwich-Village types likely to support his innovative programs. Wright had a different set of aims. He wanted to apply the principles of organic architecture to the skyscraper and reinvent the building type. Wright's interest in the skyscraper dated from the start of his career, when he worked for Louis Sullivan, a pioneer skyscraper architect, and witnessed the birth of the skyscraper in Chicago in the late 1880s and 1890s. But in the late 1920s, as he endured unemployment and a critical decline, Wright considered the skyscraper with a new sense of urgency. The skyscraper was the iconic modern building type. More than a job, the New York commission offered redemption—a chance to vindicate his reputation as a modern architect.

The design of St. Mark's was a breakthrough and ranks as one of Wright's most original ideas. The project was initiated in 1927, but Wright was not called upon to produce the drawings until 1929. In the interim, Guthrie installed a more sympathetic vestry to gain support for the controversial project, and the tower simmered in Wright's mind. While retaining the cantilever structure and glass and copper wall from the National Life Insurance Company Building scheme of 1924 (Fig. 4.2), Wright introduced a centralized structure, which instigated a variety of changes in the organically unified design (Figs. 4.3, 4.4). The St. Mark's tower is defined by four central pylons and the geometry of a rotated square. The wedge-shaped pylons swing out from the corners of an inscribed central square. Like niches scooped out of crossing piers in a Renaissance church, hexagonal utility and elevator shafts are hollowed from the pylons and contain circulation in the center of the tower. Tapering into load-bearing walls, the pylons also serve to divide the tower into apartment quadrants, a compact arrangement that eliminates hallways and efficiently uses every inch of space.

The plan relates to Wright's interest in the 1920s in centralized designs. Three schemes in particular bear upon St. Mark's: the Big Tree or Wigwam Cabin for the Lake Tahoe summer colony of 1923, a rotated square plan with a fireplace that accentuates the center; the Nakoma Country Club of 1924, an octagonal pavilion with a central fireplace based on a rotated square; and the Steel Cathedral, designed in 1927 for William Norman Guthrie, an essay in hexagonal planning structured by an inner ring of pylons.[2] Like the Steel Cathedral, St. Mark's exhibits a high degree of structural expression. The pylons emerge at the top of the tower so that unlike the decorative crowns of New York's setback towers, St. Mark's is crowned with a display of structure. Wright also exposed the pylons on the ground. The bond of building and ground plane was a hallmark of Wright's architecture, and his previous skyscrapers sit squarely on the ground, but the St. Mark's tower has a pedestal base. Wright borrowed Le Corbusier's idea of the pilotis in order to expose the structure, the core which forms the organic building, and to allow a visitor to experience the cantilever principle in the entry sequence.

Each apartment in St. Mark's is a duplex, with bedrooms on the upper level overlooking a double-height living room below. Applying planning principles honed in his earlier houses, Wright positioned the entrance opposite the corner of the living room, where the space rises to two stories and the view extends beyond the glass wall. The duplex was a well-regarded apartment type. Before passing into broader usage in New York, the two-story room lit by an oversize window was introduced

2   For a discussion of these projects, see David De Long, "Frank Lloyd Wright: Designs for an American Landscape, 1922–1932," in **Frank Lloyd Wright: Designs for an American Landscape, 1922-1932**, ed. De Long (New York: Harry Abrams, 1996), 15-134.

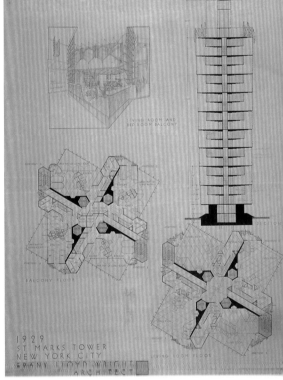

Figure 4.3 Perspective view of the St. Mark's Tower, New York City, revised project, 1929. FLWF 2905.041. © Frank Lloyd Wright Foundation.

Figure 4.4 Interior view of duplex, plans of the balcony and living room floors, and section, St. Mark's Tower, New York City, project, 1929. FLWF 2905.011. © Frank Lloyd Wright Foundation.

Figure 4.5   Charles A. Rich, Beaux Arts Studios (now called Bryant Park Studios), 80 West 40th Street at Sixth Avenue, New York City, 1901.

for artist studios (Fig. 4.5).[3] It retains this association at St. Mark's, where Guthrie's desire to attract an artistic clientele perfectly converges with Wright's formal exploration of rotational geometry and a triangular module. The bedroom floor in St. Mark's is rotated thirty degrees; it runs diagonally across the living room then cuts through the wall, expressing the rotation in the form of a small outdoor terrace. Whereas Le Corbusier's duplex interiors are contained in smooth cubic boxes, the expressive structure, rotational spin, and varied materials of the St. Mark's tower create a faceted, richly textured exterior. Extending with the structural pylons are exterior projections built in reinforced concrete—kitchenettes and bathrooms on one axis, fire stairs and balconies on the other—and bands of patterned copper panels demarcate the duplex floors.

St. Mark's shows that Wright carefully studied and learned from Le Corbusier's highrise ideas; this is clear from the pedestal base as well as two larger-scale planning moves which are influenced by *Ville Contemporaine*. Unlike Wright's earlier towers that follow the lot lines, St. Mark's introduces a freestanding tower in a park setting.[4] Guthrie had requested only one tower, yet Wright provided four: two towers stand in the churchyard, one replaces the rectory, and another rises across the street, on the gore of Stuyvesant and 10th Streets (Cat. 9). To realize this plan, it would have been necessary to destroy the historic cemetery, the rectory built in 1900 by Ernest Flagg, and several row houses attributed to James Renwick, architect of St. Patrick's Cathedral, which is to say that Wright proposed a radical change in site conditions. It is also significant that despite the limited scope of the commission and his opposition to high density, Wright multiplied the towers. Making four towers, however, asserted the urban dimension of the St. Mark's design, as a solo building might not have, and invited comparisons between his urban vision and that of Le Corbusier.

In one of its signal achievements, the St. Mark's tower brings the Machine into harmony with Nature, to use Wright's vocabulary. Wright described St. Mark's as an industrial production. His insistence on its modern materials, pre-fabricated construction, and pre-fabricated, built-in steel furniture was, in part, directed at the European functionalists. But the presiding concept of the tower is that it is like a tree. This image performs several functions. It explains the cantilever principle: the floors project from the central supports like branches from a trunk. It evokes Wright's aspiration to reinsert nature in the city: the apartment dweller can see the sky, enjoy plentiful light, and walk outdoors onto plant-draped terraces, two per apartment. And the image encapsulates the core principle of organic architecture.

Intrigued by a different aspect of the St. Mark's tower, the *Architectural Record* commended Wright for realizing "some of the most advanced aims professed by European architects."[5] As this editorial comment suggests, the tower was a marker of Wright's modernity at a time when his credentials as a modernist were under attack, and it registers his serious engagement with Le Corbusier's ideas. The pedestal base, or pilotis, the freestanding tower, and the park setting derive from Le Corbusier, but Wright used these ideas in a thoroughly original manner to elaborate his idea of a centralized, cantilever structure. The wonder of the creative process is that some rejected, even anathematized ideas nevertheless spurred Wright to realize his idea of organic architecture in the vertical dimension.

3 Other noteworthy duplex apartment buildings in New York include Charles Buckham's Gainsborough Studios of 1908 on Central Park South, and Charles Platt's Studio Building of 1905-06, at 131-135 East 66th Street at the corner of Lexington Avenue. On duplex apartments, see the excellent discussion in Robert A. M. Stern, Gregory Gilmartin, and John Massengale, **New York 1900: Metropolitan Architecture and Urbanism 1890-1915** (New York: Monacelli Press, 1983), 295-99; Keith N. Morgan, **Charles A. Platt: The Artist as Architect** (New York: Architecture History Foundation; and Cambridge, Mass.: MIT Press, 1985), 142-45; and Elizabeth Collins Cromley, **Alone Together: A History of New York's Early Apartments** (Ithaca: Cornell University Press, 1999), 166-171.

4 It should also be noted that like the church, the towers are aligned with Stuyvesant Street, which runs on a diagonal. By turning off the street grid, the towers echo the rotational geometry of the interior plan and capture more sunlight for the apartments.

5 "The Glass House for America: Saint Mark's Towers, Frank Lloyd Wright Architect," **Architectural Record** 67 (January 1930): 1.

Modern Architecture

The St. Mark's commission was advancing when Princeton University invited Wright to deliver the Kahn Lectures, a distinguished series named for their benefactor Otto Kahn. Wright proposed to give six instead of the requested eight lectures and to organize a comprehensive exhibition of his work to date. "In six days the world was made. The seventh the work was visible….," Wright teased in making a counter-offer. Wright was contacted in February 1930; the exhibition and lectures took place three months later, from May 6–14, 1930. Far from complaining about short notice, Wright seemed to consider it good timing, an opportunity to reintroduce himself to the American public.

The Kahn Lectures came at a time when Wright's reputation was under attack. In a series of widely disseminated writings beginning in 1928, Henry-Russell Hitchcock announced that Wright was "the end of a line." Surveying the diversity of recent architecture and inventing a clear story line, Hitchcock identified two partially sequential, partially opposing camps: the New Traditionalists, whom he politely admired for achievements decidedly in the past; and the New Pioneers, to whom the future belonged. He viewed Wright as a New Traditionalist, more a creature of nineteenth-century picturesque than the modern machine age. His theories were contradictory and incomplete, his approach "complicated with Nature worship," his influence over.[6] While acknowledging Wright's prophetic role as a "founder of a tradition much followed in Europe," Hitchcock regarded modern architecture as a European invention and anointed Le Corbusier as leader of the New Pioneers.[7] "Why new?" Wright belittled the redundancy of the critic's phrase. "A pioneer is a pioneer, *n'est-ce pas*?"[8]

Hitchcock's dismissal coincided with the English translation in 1927 of Le Corbusier's influential book *Towards a New Architecture*, which captured public attention and reinforced Wright's eclipse. The book was not Wright's first encounter with Le Corbusier. Europeans in his studio knew the work, and in 1925, the architect's son Lloyd designed a cruciform skyscraper intersected by highways based on Le Corbusier's *Ville Contemporaine* (1922). But *Towards a New Architecture* provided a fuller picture and gave Wright a target of attack. In September 1928 he published a short, scorching review. "The fact that all Le Corbusier says or means was at home here in architecture in America in the work of Louis Sullivan and myself—more than twenty-five years ago, and is fully on record in both building and writing here and abroad, has no meaning for him…."[9] Le Corbusier discovered "the surface effects best suited to the time," but his machine aesthetic was too literal and lacks "the quality of depth that alone … makes the building no less organic than the tree itself."[10] Wright's reading of the manifesto stirred a highly creative response in the St. Mark's tower, his organic tower-tree. The Princeton project manifests the same spirit of rebuttal and fierce intention to arrest his critical decline.

Of the three parts of the multimedia Princeton engagement—exhibition, lectures and their publication as a book—Wright was most interested in the exhibition of his work, the first since 1914, and took responsibility for curating the show. He selected the material to display, specified new models, designed demountable stands so that the exhibition could more easily travel, and organized the travel

6 Henry-Russell Hitchcock, Jr., **Modern Architecture: Romanticism and Reintegration** (New York: Payson and Clarke, 1929; reprint 1993), 104, 114, 117. Hitchcock previously advanced this view in "Modern Architecture. I. The Traditionalists and the New Tradition," **Architectural Record** vol. 63 (April 1928): 337-49; "Modern Architecture. II. The New Pioneers," **Architectural Record** vol. 63 (May 1928): 453-460; and Frank Lloyd Wright, **Les Maitres de l'Architecture** (Paris, 1928). Hitchcock's perspective also shaped the Museum of Modern Art's landmark exhibition on modern architecture in 1932.

7 Henry-Russell Hitchcock, Jr., "Modern Architecture. I. The Traditionalists and the New Tradition," **Architectural Record** vol. 63 (April 1928): 340.

8 Frank Lloyd Wright, "In the Cause of Architecture: Purely Personal" (unpublished, 1928), in **Frank Lloyd Wright Collected Writings** vol. 1, ed. Bruce Brooks Pfeiffer (New York: Rizzoli, 1992), 255.

9 Frank Lloyd Wrigh, "Towards a New Architecture," **World Unity** II/6 (September 1928): 393; reprinted in **Frank Lloyd Wright Collected Writings** vol. 1, ed. Bruce Brooks Pfeiffer, 317-18. Horace Holley, managing editor of *World Unity*, was a member of the vestry of St. Mark's. Guthrie put him on the vestry to help push through Wright's building project.

10 Ibid., 318.

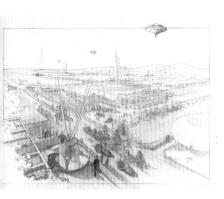

Figure 4.10 Broadacre City, unpublished rendering for *A Living City*, 1958. FLWF 5825.004. © Frank Lloyd Wright Foundation

effective. For his part, he traveled to Princeton to see the exhibition, in particular the St. Mark's model, and to consult university engineers about the viability of a cantilever tower. The engineers endorsed the structure and told Guthrie it would stand, but Guthrie lost his former courage:

"I did not expect that you would propose an entirely original process…so radical a departure—one might rather say…revolution…," he wrote Wright in a confessional letter. "It may seem quite mad to you, who are filled to the brim with enthusiasm for the ideal project; but I have been mentally wrestling all by myself with insistent doubts of the practicality of your proposal. The model removed my ignorance. I saw that your structure was self-evident, but you did not seem to have reckoned with our persistent human nature…Glass houses—stones, of course, suggested at once! How would any one feel safe?… Stone and brick give a feeling of security, and that feeling is what one must have in a house, if it is to operate as a home. The glass extending from ceiling to floor? I am assailed at once with vertigo. If there is not up to the waist at least, the feel of the solid wall, a considerable percentage [of tenants] will have a strong impulse to commit suicide."[23]

St. Mark's precarious finances combined with the cyclic building downturn and national depression obliged Guthrie to pursue a more prudent endowment campaign. Beauty and originality will "win out in the long run…," he reassured himself as much as Wright, "but one must be very strong financially to be allowed to make even the start."[24]

Harold Price met this precondition.

Field Trip
Once the project ended, the St. Mark's towers assumed a new role in Broadacre City and enjoyed a long afterlife as a theoretical project. Championing the isolated tower in *The Disappearing City* (1932), another theoretically oriented book, Wright allowed that "tall buildings are not barred" from the new city, but insisted that "they must stand free in natural parks."[25] Broadacre was based on a principle that a skyscraping tower inherently refutes: "What is any building as architecture without an intimate relation to the ground?"[26] Still Wright advocated his recent invention and the necessity of vertical form.

In 1934, working with a team of apprentices of the recently established Taliesin Fellowship during a winter session in Chandler, Arizona, Wright created a large model of Broadacre City representing an area of four square miles and accommodating 1400 families. Upon completion the model toured the country, beginning in April–May 1935 at Rockefeller Center, perhaps Wright's favorite urban target. Everything wrong with American cities could be seen in Rockefeller Center, because of its construction—unnecessarily heavy masonry cladding on steel frames—because the Center failed to reduce congestion, and because the much vaunted complex fell short of Wright's aspiration to bring nature into the city. Broadacre City and the St. Mark's Tower were Wright's critique of Rockefeller Center. An installation photograph shows the provocative models which stood side by side (Fig. 4.8). In fact, numerous miniature versions of the tower were scattered across Broadacre to demonstrate proper siting of the skyscraper, no longer an urban form. Nearly invisible in aerial views of the model, the slender towers become salient in photographs at lower angles (Fig. 4.9). After the inaugural tour of the Broadacre exhibition in 1935, the model returned to Taliesin where it was a

23 William Norman Guthrie to FLW, 20 May 1930. Columbia University, Avery Architectural and Fine Arts Library, Drawings and Archives, 106.7.5.

24 Ibid.

25 Frank Lloyd Wright. **The Disappearing City** (New York: W. F. Payson, 1932), 45.

26 Ibid., 40.

work in progress and subject of several subsequent books: *Architecture and Modern Life* (1938), *When Democracy Builds* (1945), and *The Living City* (1958). (Fig. 4.10; see also Fig. 1.36, Cat. 39)

As Wright passed his ninetieth birthday, the St. Mark's vision remained elusive. The Johnson Research Tower (1943–50), the first tower Wright managed to build, was based on the cantilever principle, but it bears no resemblance to the St. Mark's model. The Johnson Research Tower is a laboratory with a columnar structure, not an apartment building based on the spokes of a square. A genuinely site-specific work, its materials (Pyrex tubing and brick), streamlined look, location and proportions were dictated by Wright's earlier Administration Building. One understands, as Wright began to face his own mortality, that he had a pent-up desire, after such intensive exploration, to build the long deferred St. Mark's tower.

Since Harold Price wanted an office building, Wright had to revise the St. Mark's design. He replaced three of the four quadrants with one-story offices shaded by horizontal louvers, leaving apartments in the southwest corner where the light and views were best. This programmatic change led to several others that dissolved the basic symmetry of the New York scheme. The Price Tower has one exterior stair, separate entrances for residents and office workers, a penthouse suite, and rooftop garden. As a result of these adjustments, every side of Price Tower is different, a complexity that induces you to walk around it and admire its changing, freestanding form.

The Price Tower is an aesthetic triumph which may excuse its functional shortcomings, but the shortcomings are more than a matter of inadequate closet space; they are linked to Wright's way of thinking. His argument for skyscrapers in Broadacre City was based on formal grounds. As Wright reiterated in the Mile High, his final skyscraper vision from 1958, he admired super height and embraced the skyscraper as symbolic form and engineering feat. However, the idea of the skyscraper as a social form, a framework of concentrated urban sociability that has value—this he failed to understand. There is no social framework or economic rationale for a tower in a low-rise landscape. This blindness to the skyscraper as a social artifact helps to explain Wright's disregard for conditions in Bartlesville, which had no demand for highrise living, no need for the severe space efficiency of Wright's duplex studios, no advantage in small office cells for the Price Company.

Wright, at least, was not satisfied to end his skyscraper journey in small-town Bartlesville. On the basis of what may have been a casual, and now undocumented, inquiry, he worked up glamorous renderings in gold ink of one more tower, the final variant of St. Mark's. In 1956, while Price Tower was under construction, Wright designed the Golden Beacon for a site on Chicago's Lake Shore Drive (Cat. 38). At fifty stories and a height of 482 feet, the Golden Beacon is a taller version of the diminutive, nineteen-story Price Tower, which topped off at 186 feet (not including the 35-foot spire). Apart from dining clubs and a television studio on the top, the Golden Beacon was dedicated to residential use, the horizontal blades in this instance differentiating one-story apartments from vertically accentuated duplexes. On the edge of Lake Michigan and beside Lincoln Park, perched between urban and natural splendor, the Golden Beacon recast Price Tower for a genuinely urban setting. The pilgrimage of Wright's tower ended after all in Chicago, where Wright's serious thinking about urban form originally began. ■ ■ ■

EXHIBITION CATALOGUE

Mónica Ramírez-Montagut

- All designs by Frank Lloyd Wright unless otherwise noted.
- Objects belonging to the Frank Lloyd Wright Foundation noted FLWF.
- Dimensions in inches unless otherwise noted.
- Complete selected references in Selected Bibliography.

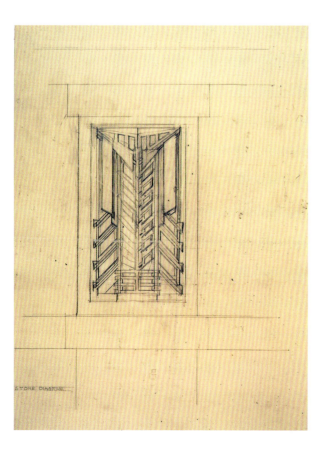

1. Larkin Company Administration Building
Buffalo, New York, 1903
(demolished 1950)
Cast ornament detail
Pencil on tracing paper
22 x 16
FLWF 0403.166

Commissioned by John Durant Larkin (1845-1926) for his mail-order company. The building was divided in three major activity areas, with a central workroom atrium surrounded by balconies and filled with natural light. **Previously not published or exhibited.**

2. **Avery and Queene Ferry Coonley Residence**
Riverside, Illinois, 1907
Monogrammed bronze plate to be set into the terrace to show orientation
Pencil on tracing paper
18 x 15
FLWF 0803.042

Residence commissioned by Avery Coonley, a Chicago industrialist, and his wife Queene Ferry of the Detroit Ferry Seed Co.
Exhibitions: New York, NY (1994).
Selected References: Bruce Brooks Pfeiffer (Studies, 1985). Frank Lloyd Wright / Frank Lloyd Wright Foundation (1991). Terence Riley / Peter Reed (1994).

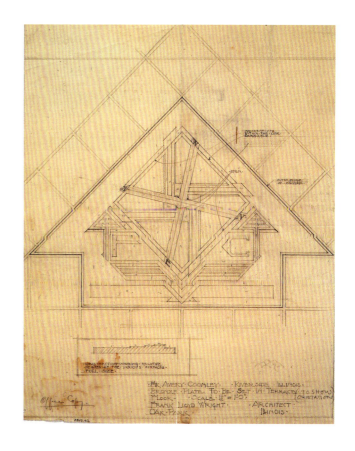

3. **Price Tower**
Bartlesville, Oklahoma, 1952-1956
Detail of monogrammed floor medallion
Dated Dec. 8, 1953
Pencil, red pencil and red ink on tracing paper
23 x 21
FLWF 5215.117

Detail of bronze floor medallion with H.C. Price Co. logo.
Previously not published or exhibited.

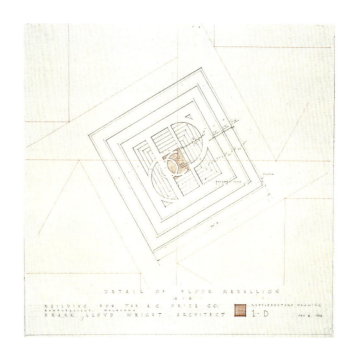

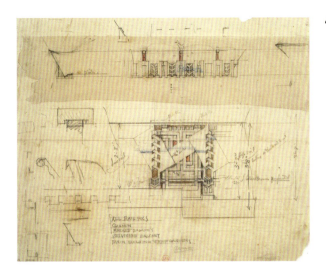

4. **Midway Gardens**
Chicago, Illinois, 1913-14
(demolished 1929)
*Detail of railings for the garden,
arcade, balconies, main building
and roof gardens*
*Color pencil and pencil on tracing
paper*
15 x 20
FLWF 1401.081

Commissioned by Edward C.
Waller, Jr., the gardens were
located where Midway
Pleasance meets Washington
Park. The gardens functioned
year-round. The Summer
Gardens featured open-air dining
and dancing while the interior
Winter Gardens provided the
same for inclement weather con-
ditions. Both areas were adorned
with sculptures by Alfonso
Ianelli.
Exhibitions: New York, NY
(1940-1941). Florence, Italy /
Zurich, Switzerland / Paris,
France / Rotterdam, Netherlands
(1951-1954) and Mexico City,
Mexico / New York, NY / Los
Angeles, CA (1951-1954). Taliesin,
Spring Green, WI / Taliesin West,
Scottsdale, AZ (1980, 1982). New
York, NY (1994).
Selected References: Frank
Lloyd Wright / Frank Lloyd
Wright Foundation (1991). Frank
Lloyd Wright / Bruce Brooks
Pfeiffer (1992). Terence Riley /
Peter Reed (1994). Frank Lloyd
Wright / Edgar Kaufman Jr.
(1998).

5. **Imperial Hotel**
Tokyo, Japan, 1914-1922 (demol-
ished 1968)
Designs for the Peacock chair
*Pencil and color pencil and on
tracing paper*
10 x 17-1/4
FLWF 1509.057

The Imperial Hotel was a three-
story hotel constructed with Oya
lava stone, precast blocks, and
tiles. The hotel featured 250
guest-rooms, sixteen private din-
ing rooms, a 300-seat cabaret,
and a 1,000-seat theater among
its hospitality options.
Exhibitions: Taliesin, Spring
Green, WI / Taliesin West,
Scottsdale, AZ (1981, 1985).
Phoenix, AZ (1990).
Selected References: Frank
Lloyd Wright / Frank Lloyd
Wright Foundation (1984). Bruce
Brooks Pfeiffer (Studies, 1985).
Bruce Brooks Pfeiffer (1990).
Frank Lloyd Wright / Frank Lloyd
Wright Foundation (1991).

6. **National Life Insurance
Building**
Chicago, 1925 (project)
*Exterior perspective of the 24-
story building*
Color pencil on tracing paper
45-5/8 x 30-1/4
FLWF 2404.001

Commissioned by Alfred Mussey
Johnson, president of the
National Life Insurance
Company, to be located at the
North Michigan Avenue over-
looking the Water Tower Square.
Exhibitions: Amsterdam,
Netherlands / Brussels,
Antwerp, Belgium / Berlin,
Germany (1931). New York, NY
(1940-1941). New York, NY (1962).
Taliesin, Spring Green, WI /
Taliesin West, Scottsdale, AZ
(1987). Phoenix, AZ (1990). New
York, NY (2004).
Selected References: Edgar
Kaufman Jr. (1955). Arthur
Drexler (1962). Bruce Brooks
Pfeiffer (1984). Bruce Brooks
Pfeiffer (Monograph, 1985).
Bruce Brooks Pfeiffer (1990).
Bruce Brooks Pfeiffer (1991).
David G. De Long (1998).

7. Skyscraper Regulation
1926 (project)
Urban development elevation
Ink on paper
17-3|4 x 32-3|4
FLWF 2603.001

Hypothetical city design of sky-scrapers with unobstructed views overlooking open space and a 24-lane roadway for fast-flowing traffic and vast parking lots.

Exhibitions: Amsterdam, Netherlands / Brussels, Antwerp, Belgium / Berlin, Germany (1931). Florence, Italy / Zurich, Switzerland / Paris, France / Rotterdam, Netherlands (1951-1954) and Mexico City, Mexico / New York, NY / Los Angeles, CA (1951-1954). New York, NY (1962). Taliesin, Spring Green, WI / Taliesin West, Scottsdale, AZ (1986). Phoenix, AZ (1990). New York, NY (2004).

Selected References:
Giuseppe Samona / Bear Run Foundation (1959). Arthur Drexler (1962). Alberto Izzo / Camillo Gubitossi (1976). Bruce Brooks Pfeiffer (Treasures, 1985). Bruce Brooks Pfeiffer (Monograph, 1985). Bruce Brooks Pfeiffer (1990). Bruce Brooks Pfeiffer (1991). Frank Lloyd Wright / Bruce Brooks Pfeiffer (1992). Jonathan Lipman / Kisho Kurokawa (1991). Bruce Brooks Pfeiffer (1999).

8. St. Mark's-in-the-Bouwerie
New York City 1929 (project)
Exterior perspective of the apart-
ment tower
Ink on paper
39 x 23-3/4
FLWF 2905.002

Commissioned in 1929 by the Reverend William Norman Guthrie, rector of St. Mark's-in-the-Bouwerie. A rental apartment building proposal to financially rescue the church. Nonetheless, the design proved to be too risky for Guthrie, who ended the project in 1930.
Exhibitions: New York, NY (1962). Taliesin, Spring Green, WI / Taliesin West, Scottsdale, AZ (1981). Phoenix, AZ (1990). Paris, Palais de Chaillot, France (1997). New York, NY (2004).
Selected References: Arthur Drexler (1962). Bruce Brooks Pfeiffer (1986). Bruce Brooks Pfeiffer (1990).

9. St. Mark's-in-the-Bouwerie
New York City 1929 (project)
Exterior perspective of the towers
Pencil on tracing paper
8-3/8 x 15-3/8
FLWF 2905.028

Exhibitions: Taliesin, Spring Green, WI / Taliesin West, Scottsdale, AZ (1980-1988). New York, NY (1994). New York, NY (2004).
Selected References: Bruce Brooks Pfeiffer (1986). Terence Riley / Peter Reed (1994). David G. De Long (1998).

10. St. Mark's-in-the-Bouwerie
New York City 1929 (project)
Interior residence view
Pencil on tracing paper
20 x 19
FLWF 2905.030

Exhibitions: none
Selected References: Bruce Brooks Pfeiffer (1986). Frank Lloyd Wright / Frank Lloyd Wright Foundation (1991).

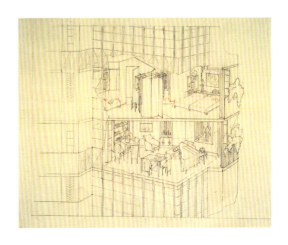

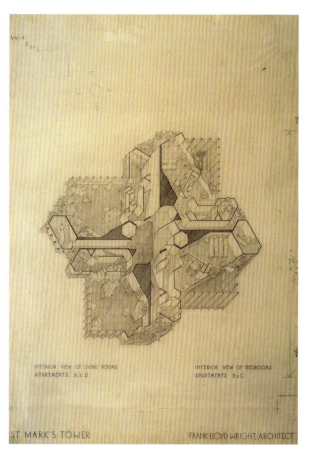

11.   **St. Mark's-in-the-Bouwerie**
New York City 1929 (project)
Interior view of the apartments
Pencil on tracing paper
34 x 24
FLWF 2905.039

Interior view of living rooms,
apartments A & D. Interior view
of bedrooms, apartments B & C.
Exhibitions: Phoenix, AZ (1990).
Selected References: Frank
Lloyd Wright (1938). Edgar
Kaufman Jr. (1955). Bruce
Brooks Pfeiffer (1990).

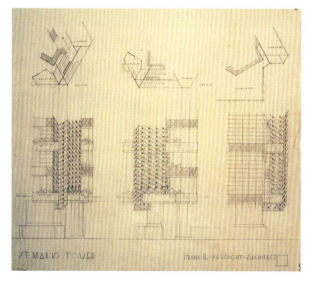

12.   **St. Mark's-in-the-Bouwerie**
New York City 1929 (project)
Copper sheets placement
Pencil on tracing paper
23 x 26
FLWF 2905.044

Exterior view of copper sheet
ornament placement and distri-
bution with partial floor plans
and elevations.
Exhibitions: none
Selected References: Frank
Lloyd Wright / Frank Lloyd
Wright Foundation (1985). Bruce
Brooks Pfeiffer (1986). Frank
Lloyd Wright / Frank Lloyd
Wright Foundation (1991).

13. **Grouped Towers**
Chicago, 1930 (project)
Apartment towers
Pencil on paper
19 x 26
FLWF 3001.001

Urban plan developed from a grouping of five of the St. Mark's tower units, but with six apartments per floor and 24 stories. It was to be located along Pearson Street looking east with Lake Michigan in the background.
Exhibitions: Florence, Italy / Zurich, Switzerland / Paris, France / Rotterdam, Netherlands (1951-1954) and Mexico City, Mexico / New York, NY / Los Angeles, CA (1951-1954). New York, NY (1962). Phoenix, AZ (1990). New York, NY (1994). New York, NY (2004).
Selected References: Henry-Russell Hitchcock (1942). Edgar Kaufman Jr. (1955). Arthur Drexler (1962). Bruce Brooks Pfeiffer (Monograph, 1985). Bruce Brooks Pfeiffer (1990). Frank Lloyd Wright / Bruce Brooks Pfeiffer (1992). Terence Riley / Peter Reed (1994). David G. De Long (1998).

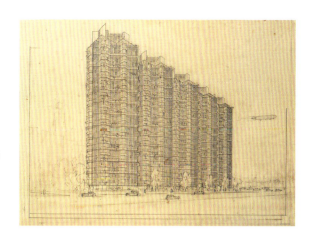

14. **Century of Progress**
1931 (project)
Elevation of skyscraper designed
for Chicago World's Fair
Pencil on paper
28 x 28-1/4
FLWF 3103.002

Designed for the Chicago Fair which represented the century of progress that had taken place between 1833 and 1933 showing the gigantic structures, methods, and materials newly available over that past century.
Exhibitions: Florence, Italy / Zurich, Switzerland / Paris, France / Rotterdam, Netherlands (1951-1954) and Mexico City, Mexico / New York, NY / Los Angeles, CA (1951-1954). New York, NY (1962).
Selected References: Arthur Drexler (1962). Bruce Brooks Pfeiffer (1986). Frank Lloyd Wright / Bruce Brooks Pfeiffer (1993).

15. **Crystal Heights**
Washington, DC, 1940
(project)
Elevation
Color pencil, pencil and sepia ink
on paper
13-3/4 x 36
FLWF 4016.003

Project commissioned by Roy S. Thurman for a hotel of 1,000 rooms, residential apartments, shops, parking garages, and a 1,000-seat theatre. The design is an offshoot of the St. Mark's tower with exteriors of copper, glass, and louvers of copper.
Exhibitions: New York, NY (1940-1941). New York, NY (1962). Taliesin, Spring Green, WI / Taliesin West, Scottsdale, AZ (1980,1988).
Selected References: Arthur Drexler (1962). Alberto Izzo / Camillo Gubitossi. (1976). Bruce Brooks Pfeiffer (1986).

16. **Crystal Heights**
Washington, DC, 1940
(project)
Exterior perspective
Ink and ink wash on tracing paper
20-1/4 x 34
FLWF 4016. 004

Exhibitions: New York, NY (1940-1941). New York, NY (1962). New York, NY (2004).
Selected References: Henry-Russell Hitchcock (1942). Arthur Drexler (1962). Alberto Izzo / Camillo Gubitossi (1976). Olgivanna Lloyd Wright (1982). Bruce Brooks Pfeiffer (1984). Bruce Brooks Pfeiffer (1986). Frank Lloyd Wright / Bruce Brooks Pfeiffer (1988). Frank Lloyd Wright / Bruce Brooks Pfeiffer (1994). David G. De Long (1998).

17. Crystal Heights

Washington, DC, 1940
(project)
Typical plan of double unit
Ink on paper
32 x 36
FLWF 4016.009

Typical plan of double unit, publication plan, 1940.

Exhibitions: Florence, Italy / Zurich, Switzerland / Paris, France / Rotterdam, Netherlands (1951-1954) and Mexico City, Mexico / New York, NY / Los Angeles, CA (1951-1954).

Selected References: Henry-Russell Hitchcock (1942). Bruce Brooks Pfeiffer (1986). Frank Lloyd Wright / Bruce Brooks Pfeiffer (1988).

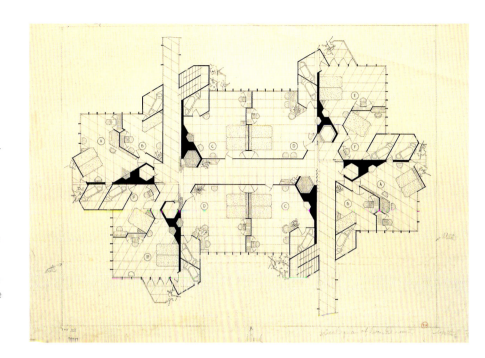

18. S.C. Johnson and Son Research Tower

Racine, Wisconsin, 1944
Section and elevation
Color pencil, pencil and sepia ink
on paper
14 x 34
FLWF 4401.099

Commissioned by Herbert (Hibbert) Johnson, president of S.C. Johnson and Son. The company began manufacturing parquet floor and evolved into producing floor paste wax.

Exhibitions: Milwaukee, WI (1992).

Selected References:
Jonathan Lipman (1986).

19. Rogers Lacy Hotel
Dallas Texas, 1946 (project)
Exterior perspective
Pencil, color pencil and ink on
tracing paper
52-3/4 x 23-7/8
FLWF 4606.001

View of the forty-seven-story
hotel for downtown Dallas, commissioned by Rogers Lacy, an oil
businessman from Texas. The
surface of the building was to
consist of diamond-shaped
panes of double-thick frosted
glass with glass-wool insulation,
allowing a softly diffused light to
permeate the interior. The main
block of the hotel houses public
rooms, shops, stores, galleries,
and guest rooms. All interior
spaces are open to sunlit balconies. A great atrium court
there rises from a cluster of
water gardens.
Exhibitions: Florence, Italy /
Zurich, Switzerland / Paris,
France / Rotterdam, Netherlands
(1951-1954) and Mexico City,
Mexico / New York, NY / Los
Angeles, CA (1951-1954). New
York, NY (1962). Phoenix, AZ
(1990). New York, NY (1994). New
York, NY (2004).
Selected References: Edgar
Kaufman Jr. (1955). Giuseppe
Samona / Bear Run Foundation
(1959). Arthur Drexler (1962).
Olgivanna Lloyd Wright (1977).
Bruce Brooks Pfeiffer (1984).
Bruce Brooks Pfeiffer
(Treasures, 1985). Bruce Brooks
Pfeiffer (1988). Frank Lloyd
Wright / Bruce Brooks Pfeiffer
(1988). Bruce Brooks Pfeiffer
(1990). Terence Riley / Peter
Reed (1994). David G. De Long
(1998). Bruce Brooks Pfeiffer
(1999).

20. **Rogers Lacy Hotel**
Dallas Texas, 1946 (project)
Tall section
Pencil, color pencil and ink on
tracing paper
65-3/4 x 36-1/4
FLWF 4606.002

Exhibitions: Florence, Italy /
Zurich, Switzerland / Paris,
France / Rotterdam, Netherlands
(1951-1954) and Mexico City,
Mexico / New York, NY / Los
Angeles, CA (1951-1954). New
York, NY (1994).
Selected References: Frank
Lloyd Wright (1940). Bruce
Brooks Pfeiffer (1987). Frank
Lloyd Wright / Bruce Brooks
Pfeiffer (1988). Terence Riley /
Peter Reed (1994).

VIEW FROM THE WEST
BUILDING FOR THE H.C. PRICE CO
BARTLESVILLE, OKLAHOMA
FRANK LLOYD WRIGHT ARCHITECT

21. Price Tower Bartlesville, Oklahoma, 1952-1956
Perspective drawing, view from the west
Pencil on tracing paper
28-1/2 X 34-1/2
FLWF 5215.001

Commissioned by Harold Charles Price, Sr., president of the H.C. Price Co., an oil pipeline company, the nineteen-story, multi-use Price Tower hosted not only offices and retail but also eight rental apartment residences in downtown Bartlesville, Oklahoma.
Exhibitions: New York, NY (1962). Spring Green, WI / Taliesin West, Scottsdale, AZ (1987).
Selected References: Arthur Drexler (1962). Bruce Brooks Pfeiffer (1987).

VIEW FROM THE SOUTH
BUILDING FOR THE H.C. PRICE CO.
BARTLESVILLE, OKLAHOMA
FRANK LLOYD WRIGHT, ARCHITECT

22. Price Tower Bartlesville, Oklahoma, 1952-1956
Perspective drawing, view from the south
Pencil and color pencil on tracing paper
43 x 34
FLWF 5215.004

Exhibitions: Phoenix, AZ (1990).
Selected References: H.C.Price Co (1953). Bruce Brooks Pfeiffer (1990). Frank Lloyd Wright / Bruce Brooks Pfeiffer (1995). David G. De Long (1998).

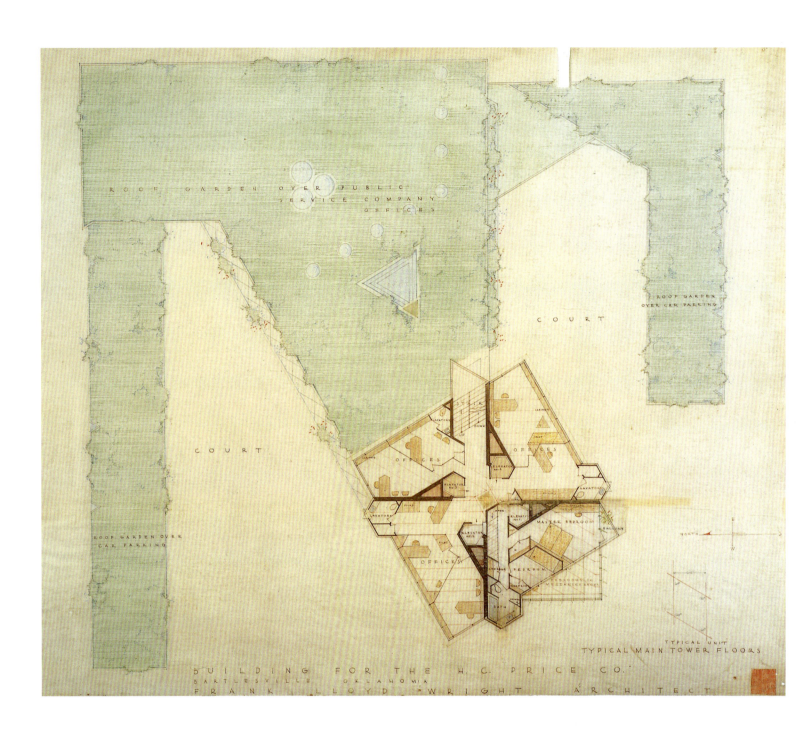

23. Price Tower Bartlesville, Oklahoma, 1952-1956
Typical footprint of one of the tower's floors
Pencil, color pencil, sepia and red ink on paper
36 x 44-3/4
FLWF 5215.005

Exhibitions: none
Selected References: Frank Lloyd Wright (1956).

LIVING ROOM

4. **Price Tower** Bartlesville, Oklahoma, 1952-1956
Interior of typical residence
Pencil and color pencil on paper
16-1/2 x 23-7/8
Signed at lower left in red square, Nov. 6 /52
FLWF 5215.007

Note that the exterior copper panels continue into the interior space to form the mezzanine balcony.
Exhibitions: Spring Green, WI / Taliesin West, Scottsdale, AZ (1980-1988).
Selected References: Bruce Brooks Pfeiffer (1988). Frank Lloyd Wright / Frank Lloyd Wright Foundation (1991). David G. De Long (1998).

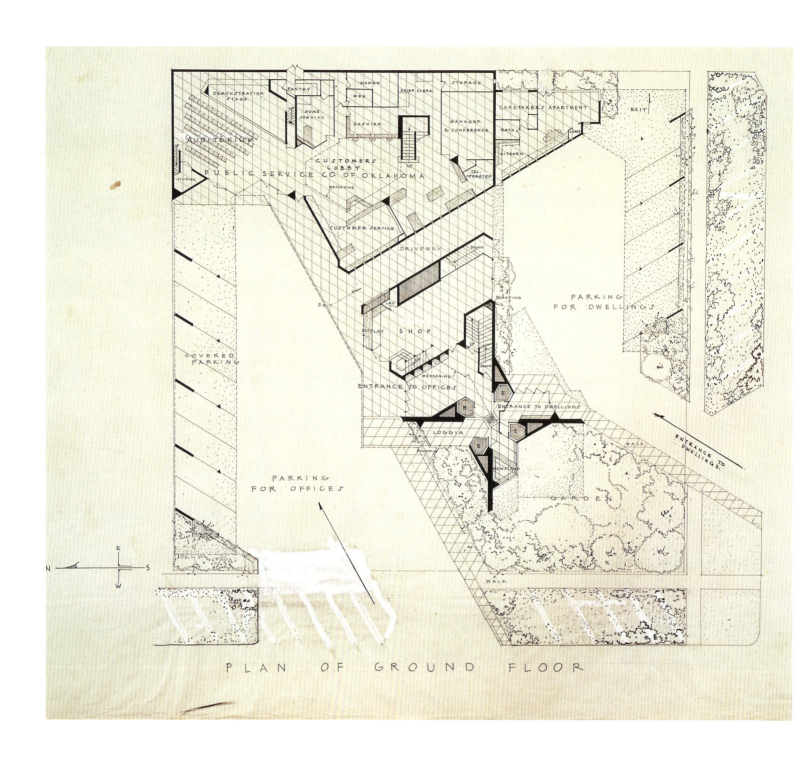

PLAN OF GROUND FLOOR

25. Price Tower Bartlesville, Oklahoma, 1952-1956
Ground floor plan
Ink on tracing paper
28 x 36
FLWF 5215.014

Ground floor plan showing access to the Public Service Co. of Oklahoma, shop, offices, and dwellings. Drawing includes final changes made to the parking design (as documented in 2.4.1956 Frank Lloyd Wright to Harold C. Price Sr. PTAC 2004.02.52a)
Exhibitions: none
Selected References: Frank Lloyd Wright (1956). Bruce Brooks Pfeiffer (1988). William Allin Storrer (1993).

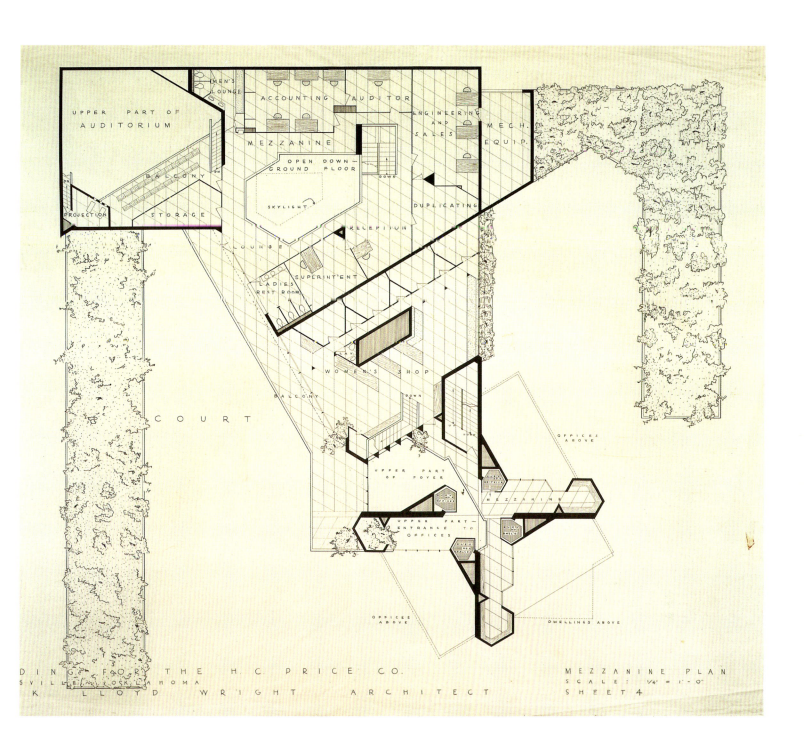

UPPER PART OF AUDITORIUM

MEN'S LOUNGE

ACCOUNTING AUDITOR

ENGINEERING AND SALES

MECH. EQUIP.

MEZZANINE

OPEN DOWN — GROUND FLOOR

DOWN

BALCONY

PROJECTION

STORAGE

SKYLIGHT

DUPLICATING

RECEPTION

LOUNGE

LADIES REST ROOM

SUPERINT'ENT

WOMEN'S SHOP

BALCONY

DOWN

COURT

UPPER PART OF FOYER

OFFICES ABOVE

MEZZANINE

UPPER PART — ENTRANCE TO OFFICES

OFFICES ABOVE

DWELLINGS ABOVE

BUILDING FOR THE H. C. PRICE CO.
BARTLESVILLE OKLAHOMA
FRANK LLOYD WRIGHT ARCHITECT

MEZZANINE PLAN
SCALE: 1/4" = 1'-0"
SHEET 4

26. **Price Tower** Bartlesville, Oklahoma, 1952-1956
Mezzanine plan
Ink on tracing paper
25 x 48
FLWF 5215.015

Exhibitions: none
Selected References: Frank Lloyd Wright (1956). Bruce Brooks Pfeiffer (1988). William Allin Storrer (1993).

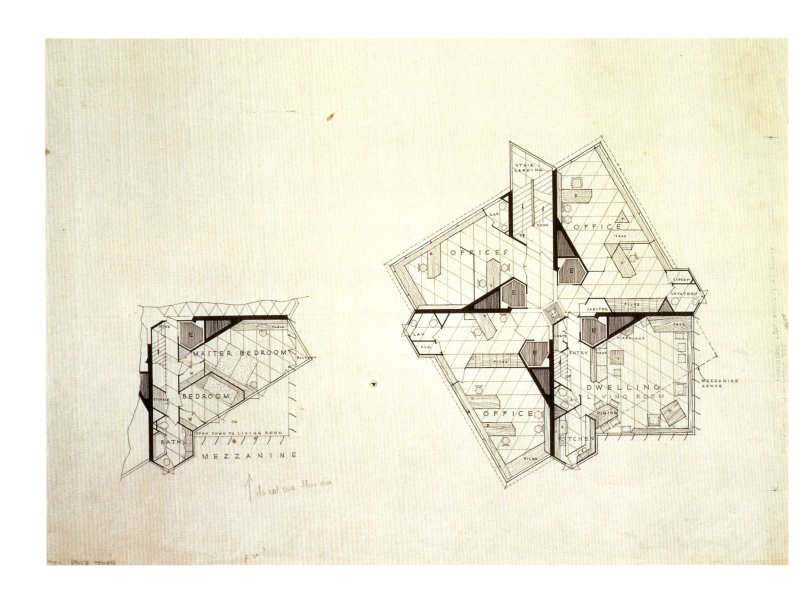

27. Price Tower Bartlesville, Oklahoma, 1952-1956
Typical tower floor plan, dwelling mezzanine
Ink on tracing paper
25-1/2 x 36
FLWF 5215.016

Exhibitions: New York, NY (1994).
Selected References: Frank Lloyd Wright (1956). Bruce Brooks Pfeiffer (1988). Jonathan Lipman / Kisho Kurokawa (1991). William Allin Storrer (1993). Terence Riley / Peter Reed (1994).

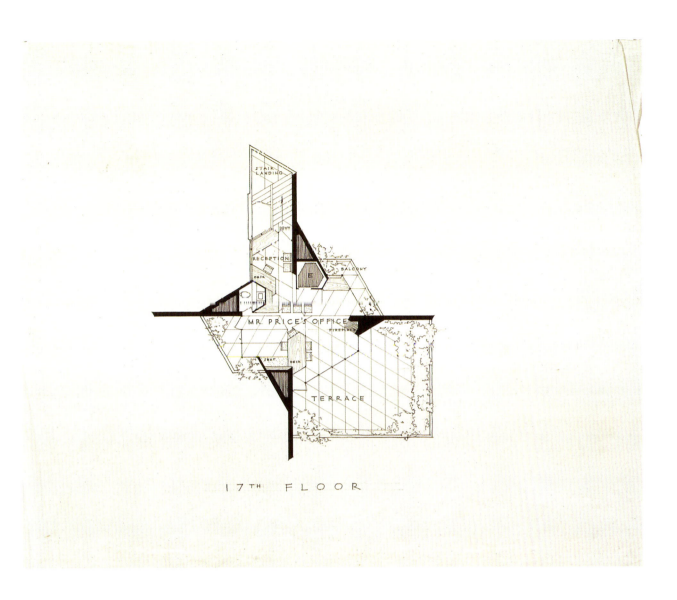

17TH FLOOR

28. **Price Tower** Bartlesville, Oklahoma, 1952-1956
Mr. Price's office, 17th floor plan (currently 19th floor)
Pencil and ink on tracing paper
25 x 36
FLWF 5215.017

Exhibitions: none
Selected References: Frank Lloyd Wright (1956). Bruce Brooks Pfeiffer (1988). William Allin Storrer (1993).

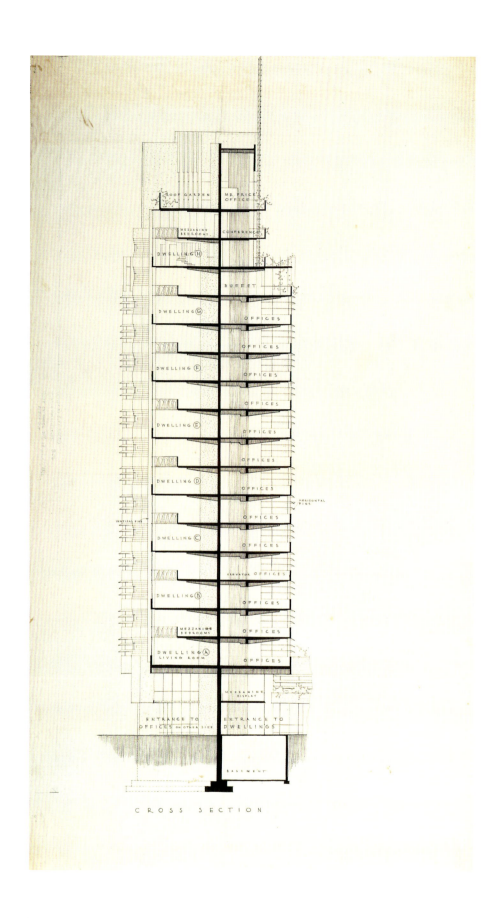

CROSS SECTION

29. **Price Tower** Bartlesville, Oklahoma, 1952-1956
Cross section
Ink on tracing paper
64-3/4 x 36
FLWF 5215.018

Exhibitions: New York, NY (1994).
Selected References: Frank Lloyd Wright (1956). Bruce Brooks Pfeiffer (1988). Jonathan Lipman / Kisho Kurokawa (1991). Terence Riley / Peter Reed (1994).

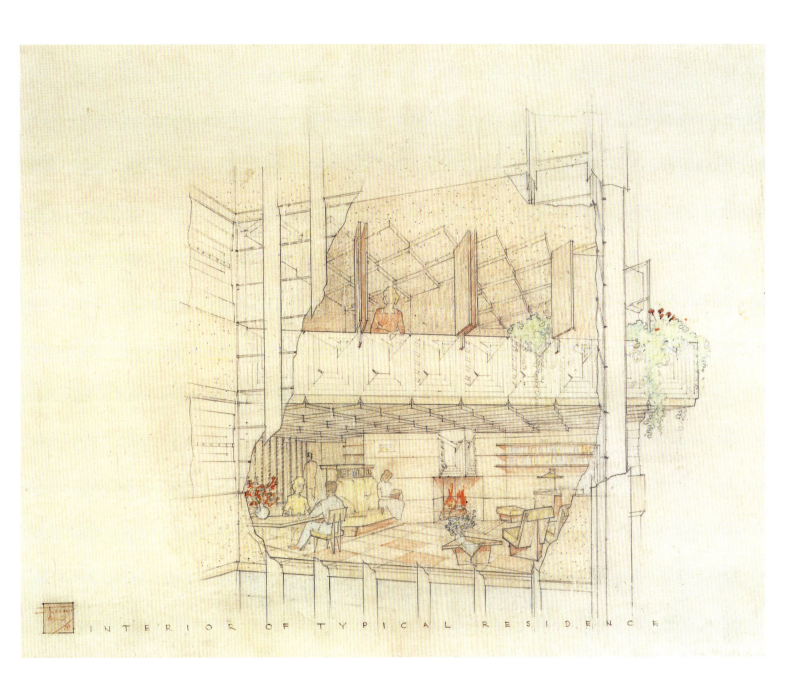

INTERIOR OF TYPICAL RESIDENCE

30. Price Tower Bartlesville, Oklahoma, 1952-1956
Interior view of an apartment
Ink and colored pencil on paper
31-5/8 X 36-1/4
FLWF 5215.185

Exhibitions: none
Selected References: Frank Lloyd Wright (1956). Bruce Brooks Pfeiffer (1988). Frank Lloyd Wright / Frank Lloyd Wright Foundation (1991).

MASTER BEDROOM

31.

31. Price Tower Bartlesville, Oklahoma, 1952-1956
Interior view of a master bedroom
Ink and colored pencil on paper
32-3/8 x 36-1/4
FLWF 5215.186

Exhibitions: none
Selected References: Frank Lloyd Wright (1956). Frank Lloyd Wright / Frank Lloyd Wright
Foundation (1991).

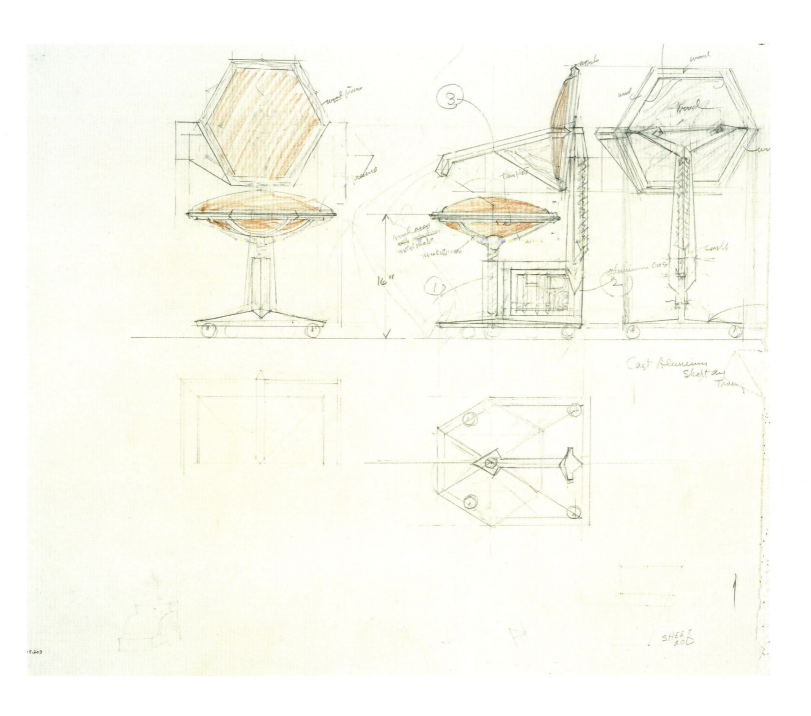

32. **Price Tower** Bartlesville, Oklahoma, 1952-1956
Working drawing for Price Tower Occasional chair
Red color pencil and pencil on tracing paper
20 x 24
FLWF 5215.203

Trolley with H.C.P.Co. logo with shaft specified in cast aluminum.
Exhibitions: none
Selected References: Bruce Brooks Pfeiffer (1987). Frank Lloyd Wright / Frank Lloyd Wright
Foundation (1991).

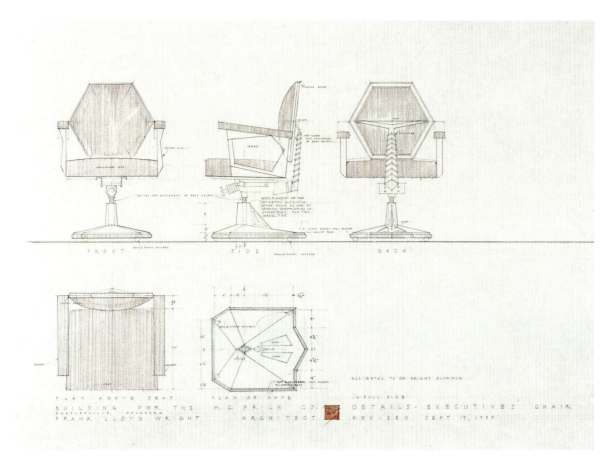

33. **Price Tower**
Bartlesville, Oklahoma,
1952-1956
*Working drawings with details for
Price Tower Executive chair
Colored red pencil and pencil on
tracing paper
25 x 36
FLWF 5215.211*

Exhibitions: none
Selected References: Frank
Lloyd Wright / Frank Lloyd
Wright Foundation (1991).

34. **Price Tower**
Bartlesville, Oklahoma,
1952-1956
*Copper panel for façade and for
interior balcony
Pencil on tracing paper
20 x 29
FLWF 5215.228*

**Previously not published or
exhibited.**

35. Point View Residences, second scheme for the Edgar J. Kaufman Charitable Trust
1953 (project)
Northwest view of apartment tower
Pencil, color pencil and sepia ink on paper
34-1/4 x 29
FLWF 5310.001

Exhibitions: New York, NY (1962). Spring Green, WI / Taliesin West, Scottsdale, AZ (1980). New York, NY (1994).

Selected References: Arthur Drexler (1962). Olgivanna Lloyd Wright (1979).Bruce Brooks Pfeiffer (1984). Bruce Brooks Pfeiffer (Treasures, 1985). Bruce Brooks Pfeiffer (1988). Frank Lloyd Wright / Bruce Brooks Pfeiffer (1995). Terence Riley / Peter Reed (1994). Frank Lloyd Wright / Edgar Kaufman Jr. Richard Cleary (1998). Bruce Brooks Pfeiffer (1999).

36. The Golden Beacon
Chicago, Illinois,
1956 (project)
Cross section of apartment tower
Pencil, color pencil, sepia and
gold ink on paper
47 x 23
FLWF 5615.003

Commissioned by Charles Glore,
the fifty-story apartment building with a restaurant on the top
floor was to be located on Lake
Shore Drive, adjacent to the
famous apartments designed by
Ludwig Mies Van der Rohe. The
lower three stories are parking
facilities.
Exhibitions: none
Selected References: Bruce
Brooks Pfeiffer (1988).

37. **The Golden Beacon**
Chicago, Illinois,
1956 (project)
Exterior perspective
Pencil, color pencil, and gold ink
on tracing paper
46-1/2 x 22-3/4
FLWF 5615.004

Exhibitions: Phoenix, AZ (1990).
New York, NY (1994). New York,
NY (2004).
Selected References:
Giuseppe Samona / Bear Run
Foundation (1959). Olgivanna
Lloyd Wright (1977). Bruce
Brooks Pfeiffer (1984). Frank
Lloyd Wright / Bruce Brooks
Pfeiffer (1988). Bruce Brooks
Pfeiffer (1990). Terence Riley /
Peter Reed (1994). Frank Lloyd
Wright / Edgar Kaufman Jr.
(1998).

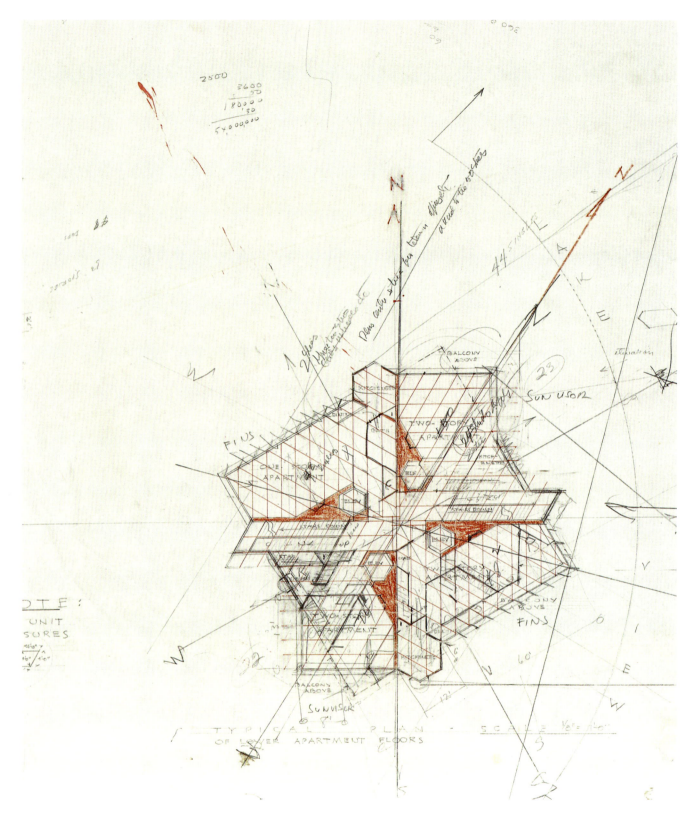

38. **The Golden Beacon**
Chicago, Illinois,
1956 (project)
Floor plan
Red pencil, pencil and red marker
on tracing paper
37 x 22
FLWF 5615.007

Typical plan of the lower
apartment floors. The module
is 4'-0" by 4'-0".
Exhibitions: none
Selected References: Bruce
Brooks Pfeiffer (1987).

39. **The Living City**
1958 (project)
(Drawings for publication)
Air view
Pencil and sepia ink on paper
36-1/4 x 42-1/4
FLWF 5825.002

Drawing for the book *The Living
City*, a revised look at Broadacre
City, portraying the city as an
integral part of the landscape.
Note that Wright includes sever-
al of his built projects.
Exhibitions: New York, NY
(1962). Spring Green, WI /
Taliesin West, Scottsdale, AZ
(1980). Tokyo, Japan / Cologne,
Germany / Mexico City, Mexico /
Chicago, IL / Los Angeles, CA
(1998-2000).
Selected References: Frank
Lloyd Wright (1958). Arthur
Drexler (1962). Alberto Izzo /
Camillo Gubitossi (1976).
Olgivanna Lloyd Wright (1982).
Bruce Brooks Pfeiffer (1984).
Frank Lloyd Wright / Bruce
Brooks Pfeiffer (1988). Claude
Massu (1990). Jonathan Lipman /
Kisho Kurokawa (1991). Frank
Lloyd Wright / Bruce Brooks
Pfeiffer (1995). David G. De Long
(1998).

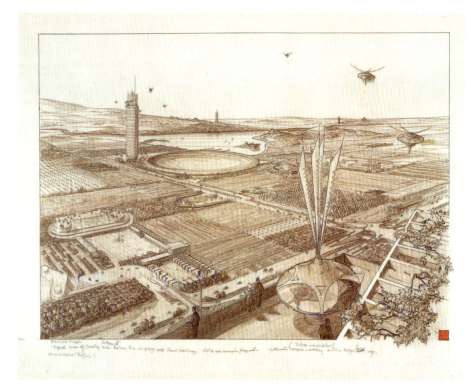

40. **Price Tower 3-D
architectural model**
1952
Original working wood model
78 x 55 x 48
FLWF 9000.010

Exhibitions: Tulsa, OK (1953).
New York, NY (1953). New York,
NY (1994). Weil am Rhein,
Germany (1998). Leipzig,
Germany / Glasgow, Scotland /
Amsterdam, Netherlands (1999) /
Dortmund, Germany (2000).
Selected References: William
Allin Storrer (2002). David G. De
Long (1998).

41. Heritage-Henredon Lounge Chair 1956
Wood and fabric, composite
31 x 30 x 35
Price Tower Arts Center
Gift of Phillips Petroleum Company, by
exchange 2004.14.1

The Heritage-Henredon Lounge Chair is from the only commercial line of furniture Frank Lloyd Wright
ever designed. This was one of two armchairs used in the Price apartment living area on the 17th floor.
Exhibitions: Bartlesville, OK (2004- to date)
Selected References: none

42. **Price Tower Desk** 1956
Ribbon Mahogany, copper and
aluminum
28 x 85 x 48
Price Tower Arts Center
Gift of Phillips Petroleum
Company 2001.01.080

Typical office desk for H.C.
Price Co. personnel, designed
by Wright in December 1954.
Exhibitions: Bartlesville, OK
(1990- to date)
Selected references: none

43. **Price Tower Desk** 1956
Ribbon Mahogany, copper and
aluminum
28 x 80 x 31-3/4
Price Tower Arts Center
Gift of Phillips Petroleum
Company 2001.01.081

Typical office desk for H.C. Price
Co. personnel, designed by
Wright in September 1954.
Exhibitions: Bartlesville, OK
(1990- to date)
Selected references: *Wright:*
Modernist 20 Century (2003).
Robert Ivy (2003). Chris Abel
(2003). Bruce Brooks Pfeiffer
(2003).

44. Price Tower Desk 1956
Ribbon Mahogany, copper and aluminum
28 x 79 x 31-1/2
Price Tower Arts Center
Gift of Etsuko and Joe Price 2004.18

Typical office desk for the H.C. Price Co. personnel, designed by Wright in September 1954. Note that the stainless steel wastepaper basket is integrated into the desk design. One example of thirty (as documented in 8.30.1956 Harold C. Price Sr. to Frank Lloyd Wright, FLWA.)
Exhibitions: none
Selected references: Robert Ivy (2003). Chris Abel (2003). Bruce Brooks Pfeiffer (2003).

45. Price Tower Desk Extension
1956
Ribbon Mahogany, copper and aluminum
25 x 41-1/2 x 20-1/4
Price Tower Arts Center
Gift of Phillips Petroleum Company 2001.01.083

Wood typing table. Typical extension for the H.C. Price Co. personnel desk.
Exhibitions: Bartlesville, OK (1990 - to date)
Selected references: none

46. Price Tower Desk Extension
1956
Ribbon Mahogany, copper and aluminum
24-1/2 x 36-3/4 x 32
Price Tower Arts Center
Gift of Phillips Petroleum Company 2001.01.084

Wood typing top affixed to a H.C. Price Co. personnel desk.
Previously not published or exhibited.

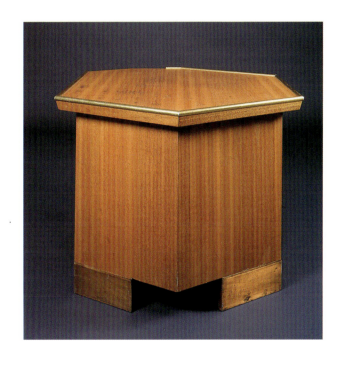

47. Price Tower Wastepaper Basket 1956
Stainless steel
12 x 16-1/4 x 6-1/2
Price Tower Arts Center
Gift of Phillips Petroleum Company 2001.01.086

Typical metal wastepaper basket designed specifically to fit the lower back end of all the H.C. Price Co. personnel desks.
Exhibitions: Bartlesville, OK (1990 - to date)
Selected references: Dixie Legler (2001).

48. Price Tower Casual Chair 1956
Cast aluminum frame with orange re-upholstery
32-3/4 x 29 x 25
Price Tower Arts Center
Gift of Phillips Petroleum Company 2001.01.003

Price Tower Casual chair (also known as Occasional or Easy chair) with arm support and back spine descending to the base of the chair. One example of forty made (as documented in 8.30.1956 Harold C. Price Sr. to Frank Lloyd Wright, FLWA). See associated drawing for this chair type and note the slightly different base in Catalogue No. 32.
Exhibitions: Bartlesville, OK (1990 - to date)
Selected references: Frank Lloyd Wright (1956). David A. Hanks (1989). William Allin Storrer (1993). Iain Thomson (1997). Timothy A. Eaton (1997). David G. De Long (1998). Robert Ivy (2003). Chris Abel (2003). Yukio Futagawa / Bruce Brooks Pfeiffer (2003).

49. **Price Tower Casual Chair** 1956
*Cast aluminum frame with white leather
re-upholstery*
32-3/4 x 28 x 24
Price Tower Arts Center
Gift of Phillips Petroleum Company 2001.01.012

Price Tower Casual chair with arm support and back spine descending to the base of the chair. One
example of forty made (as documented in 8.30.1956 Harold C. Price Sr. to Frank Lloyd Wright, FLWA.)
Exhibitions: Bartlesville, OK (1990 - to date)
Selected references: Frank Lloyd Wright (1956). David A. Hanks (1989). William Allin Storrer (1993).
Iain Thomson (1997). Timothy A. Eaton (1997). David G. De Long (1998). Wright: Modernist 20 Century
(2003). Robert Ivy (2003). Chris Abel (2003). Yukio Futagawa / Bruce Brooks Pfeiffer (2003).

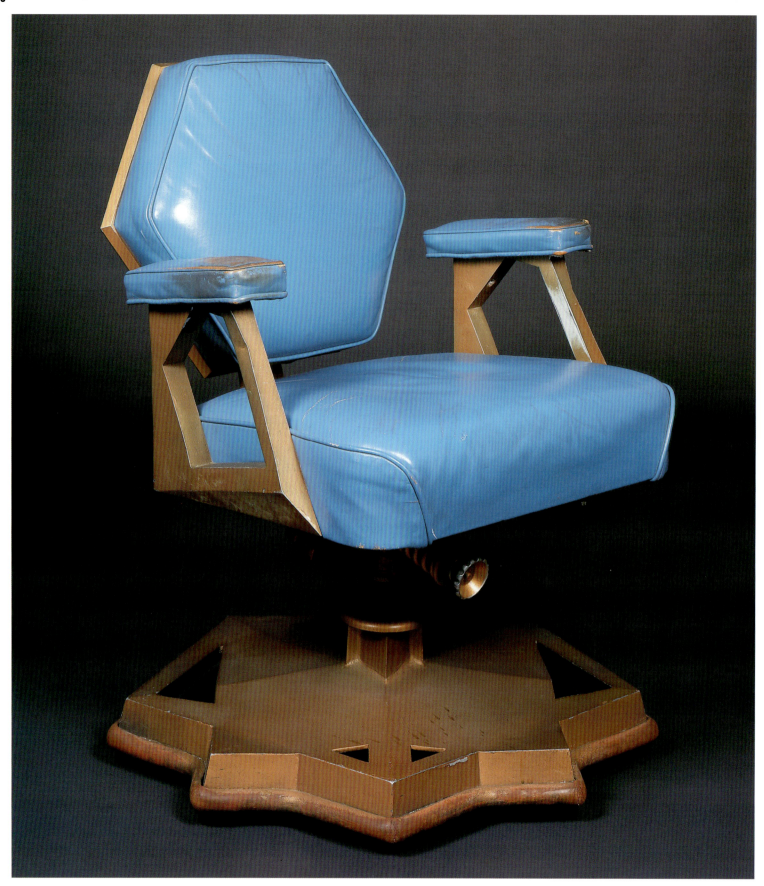

50. Price Tower Executive Armchair 1956
Cast aluminum frame with blue leather re-upholstery
34-3/4 x 28-1/2 x 26-1/2
Price Tower Arts Center
Gift of Harold C. Price, Jr. 2002.03.2

This example of the Executive chair—made for Harold C. Price, Sr.'s use in his 19th floor office—is the only one known to have been used at Price Tower (interview with Harold C. Price, Jr., March 2005). Its swivel system was manufactured by Artmetal Construction Company, Hamestown, New York, and it was specified to be bright aluminum with a rubber heel bumper (see Catalogue no. 33, FLWF 5215.211, 9.19.1955). In a letter of 12.28.1955 (FLWA), Wright himself complains that this design required more attention than the building itself.

Exhibitions: Bartlesville, OK (2001 - to date)
Selected References: Iain Thomson (1997). Iain Thompson (1999). Robert Ivy (2003). Yukio Futagawa / Bruce Brooks Pfeiffer (2003)

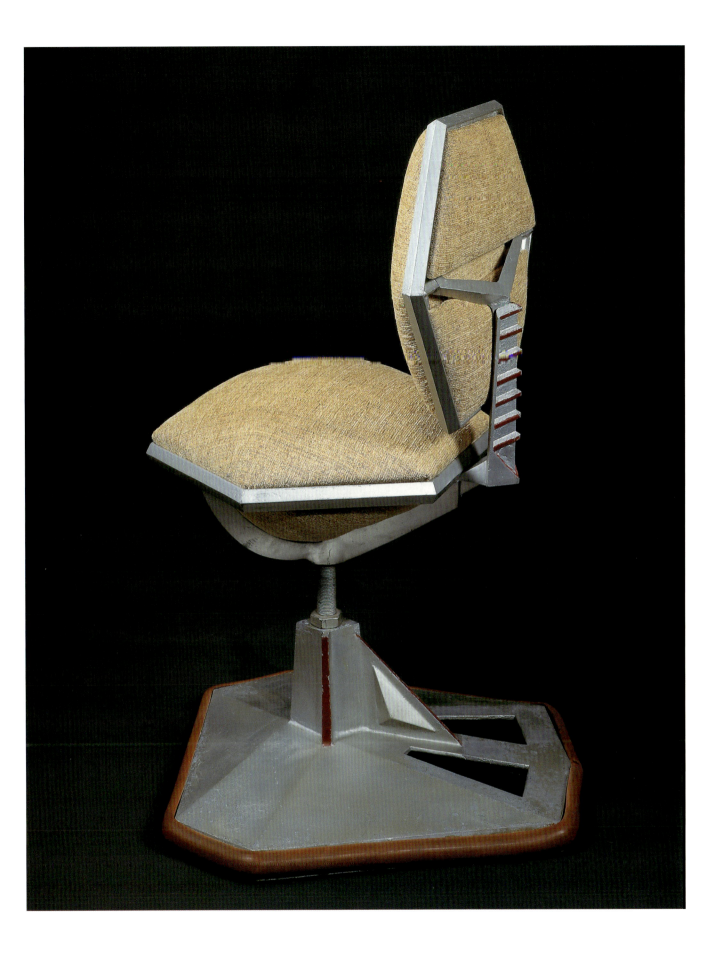

51. **Price Tower Stenographer Chair** 1956
Cast aluminum frame with granite color
re-upholstery
33-1/2 x 18-3/4 x 20-1/2
Price Tower Arts Center
Gift of Harold C. Price, Jr. 2002.03.1

Price Tower Stenographer chair with adjustable swivel seat, backrest, and no arms. One example of fourteen made (as documented in 8.30.1956 Harold C. Price Sr. to Frank Lloyd Wright, FLWA.)
Exhibitions: Bartlesville, OK (1990 - to date)
Selected References: Frank Lloyd Wright (1956). Donald Canty (1982). David A. Hanks (1989). Spencer Hart (1993). Cindy Allen (2003).

52. Price Tower Copper Table 1956
Wood structure and copper exterior, patinated
28-1/2 x 39-3/4 x 26-3/4
Price Tower Arts Center
Gift of Phillips Petroleum Company 2001.01.016

Copper-clad furniture for the 16th-floor company commissary dining area and terraces. One example of twenty tables made (as documented in 8.30.1956 Harold C. Price Sr. to Frank Lloyd Wright, FLWA.) Note the edge details are the same as Harold Price, Sr.'s desk.
Exhibitions: Bartlesville, OK (1990 - to date). Wichita, KS (2005, a similar example).
Selected References: David G. De Long (1998). Dixie Legler (2001).

53. Price Tower Copper Stools (2) 1956
Wood structure and copper exterior, patinated
15-1/2 x 19-3/4 x 17-1/4 each
Price Tower Arts Center
Gift of Phillips Petroleum Company 2001.01.025,
2001.01.028

Copper-clad furniture for the 16th-floor company commissary dining area and terraces. Two examples of forty stools made (as documented in 8.30.1956 Harold C. Price Sr. to Frank Lloyd Wright, FLWA.) Note the edge details are the same as Harold Price, Sr.'s desk.
Exhibitions: Bartlesville, OK (1990 - to date). Wichita, KS (2005, a similar example).
Selected References: David G. De Long (1998). Paige Rense (2003). Dixie Legler (2001).

54. Price Tower Copper Stool Cushion 1956
Waterproof fabric with interior foam cushion
2 x 18-1/2 x 18-1/2
Price Tower Arts Center
Gift of Phillips Petroleum Company 2001.01.037

Example of cushions made for interior and exterior purposes.
Exhibitions: Bartlesville, OK (1990 - to date). Wichita, KS (2005, a similar example).
Selected References: David G. De Long (1998). Dixie Legler (2001). Paige Rense (2003).

55. **Price Tower Coffee Table**
1956
Wood, copper and round
aluminum trim
15x 38-1/2 x 38-1/2
Price Tower Arts Center
Gift of Shin 'en Kan Foundation
2003.08.01.418

A modified version of the Lewis
Coffee Table (1939), the Price
Tower Coffee Table has a wrap-
around aluminum mold edge.
(Image shows Coffee Table in
the Price Apartment on the
17th floor in 1955).
Previously not published or
exhibited.

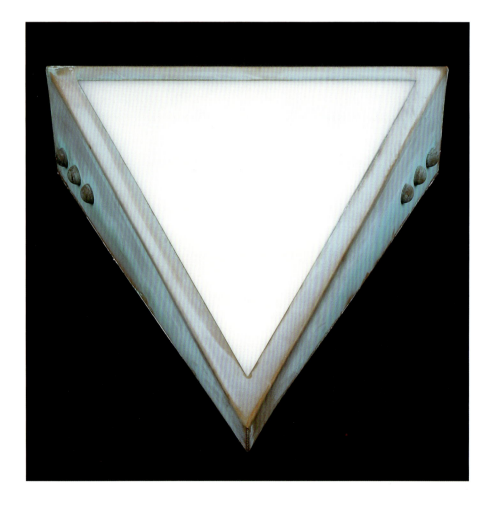

56. **Wall-mounted light fixture**
1956
Patinated copper and
translucent glass
Price Tower Arts Center
Gift of Phillips Petroleum
Company 2001.01.224
Previously not published or
exhibited.

57. H.C. Price Co. lunch plates 1956
Ceramic with HCPCo logo
10" diameter and 6" diameter
Price Tower Arts Center
Gift of Linda Caputo 2002.18.1-2002.18.2

Lunch plates for the 16th-floor company commissary and dining area of the company with the H.C. Price Co. logo designed by Wright.
Exhibitions: Bartlesville, OK (2002 - to date)
Selected References: none

58. Price Tower Copper Panel 1956
Price Tower building exterior panel, unpatinated
38-1/2 x 29-1/2 x 1-1/2
Price Tower Arts Center
Gift of Phillips Petroleum Company 2001.01.150

One example of the façade's copper panels on every other floor of the Price Tower with geometric pattern, prior to the patina treatment.
Previously not published or exhibited.

59. Price Tower Copper Panel 1956
Price Tower building exterior panel, patinated
38-1/2 x 29-1/2 x 1-1/2
Price Tower Arts Center
Gift of Phillips Petroleum Company 2001.01.148

One example of the façade's copper panels with geometric pattern and hand-patina treatment. The panels form part of the exterior façade on every other floor of the Price Tower and form the interior mezzanine balconies of the residential apartments.
Exhibitions: New York, NY (2004). Wichita, KS (2005, a similar example).
Selected References: none

**60. Price Tower Copper Louvers
(2)**, 1956
*Price Tower building louver with
patina*
26-1/2 x 19 x 2-1/2
Price Tower Arts Center
*Gift of Phillips Petroleum
Company 2001.01.163, 2001.01.164*

Two examples of the horizontal
copper louver sections that wrap
around the offices façades on
every floor of the Price Tower.
The louvers are supported by
aluminum brackets and reduce
the sun glare and air-conditioner
load.
**Previously not published or
exhibited.**

**61. Price Tower Apartment
Fireplace**, 1956
Price Tower Apartment fireplace
52 x 34 x 15
Price Tower Arts Center
*Gift of Phillips Petroleum
Company 2001.01.143.1*

Designed in January 14, 1956, the
fireplace units have pilot lights
and automatic shut off (thermo
couple) devices. Note the
stamped copper on the facia.
The sloping faces of the base are
also stamped on the edge.
(Image shows a fireplace *in situ*
in the Price Apartment on the
17th floor.)
**Previously not published or
exhibited.**

62. **Price Tower wood forms (4)** 1956
Wood
Variable dimensions
Collection of Cecil Magana

Wood forms made by the Blue Stem Foundry in Dewey, Oklahoma, for producing the sandcast aluminum Price Tower Stenographer chairs. See Catalogue No. 51.
Previously not published or exhibited.

3. **Price Tower chair spines (3)** 1956
Wood, aluminum
Variable dimensions
Collection of Cecil Magana

One wood form and two sandcast aluminum pieces that comprise the spines of the Price Tower Casual chairs. See Catalogue Nos. 48 and 49.
Previously not published or exhibited.

64. Schumacher's Taliesin Line Sample Book 1955
Printed paper and fabric samples
22-3/4 x 17-1/2 x 1-3/4
Price Tower Arts Center
Gift of Phillips Petroleum Company, by exchange
2005.01

1955 Schumacher's Taliesin Line of Decorative Fabrics and Wallpapers designed by Frank Lloyd Wright, with fabric samples specified for the Price Tower interiors.
Previously not published or exhibited.

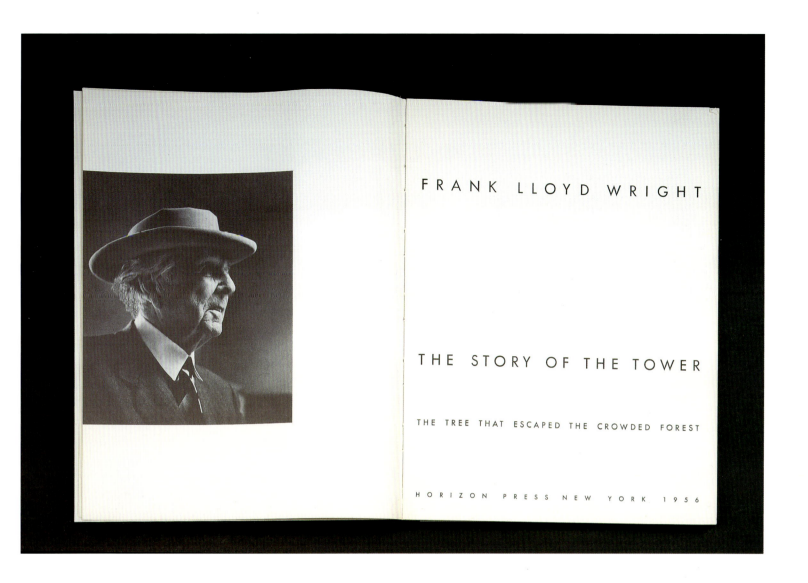

FRANK LLOYD WRIGHT

THE STORY OF THE TOWER

THE TREE THAT ESCAPED THE CROWDED FOREST

HORIZON PRESS NEW YORK 1956

5. ***The Story of the Tower***
(New York: Horizon Press, 1956)
Printed paper
11 x 9 x 3/4
Price Tower Arts Center
Gift of Mildred C. Moore 2003.09

Monograph by Frank Lloyd Wright on the Price Tower with photography by Joe Price. This example is inscribed by Frank Lloyd Wright, Harold C. Price, Sr., and Joe Price.
Exhibitions: Bartlesville, OK (2003 - to date). Wichita, KS (2005, a similar example).
Selected References: none

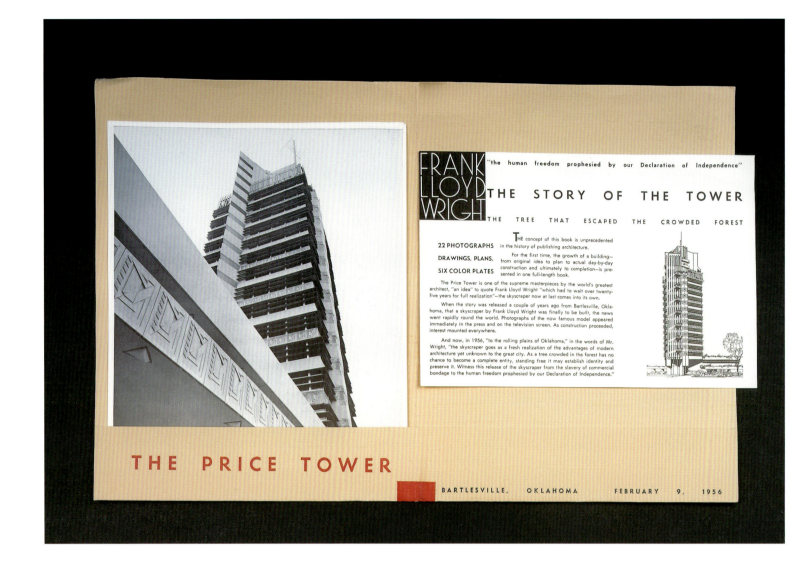

66. **Price Tower Opening Day Press Packet**
February 10th 1956
Printed paper
11 x 8-3/4 x 1/8
Price Tower Arts Center
Gift of Donald Weaver 2004.03

Press packet prepared by the H.C. Price Co. in 1956 with day and night views of the Price Tower.
Exhibitions: Bartlesville, OK (2003 - to date). Wichita, KS (2005, a similar example).
Selected References: none

57. ***Architectural Record*** 119, 1956
Printed paper
12 x 8-1/2 x 1/4
Price Tower Arts Center Archives

Periodical issue dedicated to the Price Tower, cover and pages 153-160.
Exhibitions: Bartlesville, OK (2003 - to date).
Selected References: none

68. **Selection of Price Tower Construction Film**
1952-1956
9mm color film footage (transferred to DVD system)
Price Tower Arts Center
Gift of Etsuko and Joe Price 2004.15

Color film footage of the Price Tower construction made by Joe Price from 1952 to 1956.
Previously not published or exhibited.

69. **Selection of Price Tower Photographs** 1952-1956
Black-and-white photographic prints
Dimensions variable
Price Tower Arts Center
Gift of Etsuko and Joe Price 2003.16.001 - 2003.16.297

Black-and-white photographs of the construction of the Price Tower and finished interiors made by Joe Price from 1952 to 1956.

Exhibitions: Bartlesville, OK (1990 - to date). New York, NY (2004)
Selected References: Frank Lloyd Wright (1956).

Mr. H. C. Price
The H. C. Price Company
Battlesville
Oklahoma

My dear Hal Price: I guess my telegram was ambiguous.
N.B.C. has for a month been working on me and my work as
a first in a television series:"Famous Americans". Ben
Park, Chicago, is director and he suggests your free-
skyscraper as the end of the series of buildings.

Taliesin East and West, Johnson Heliolab, Florida Southern C
College, Unity Church, etc. It would be a good start
for your advertising if you are ready.

I suggested you show drawings to Perry Prentiss of the
Architectural Forum as he is Henry Luce's man and the Life
and Time usually work together. Prentiss is very eager to
publish my work and wired me to get sight of your buildings.
Hence my telegram to you.

We are just (this coming Monday) settling down to work here.
There was much to do. Including the trip here, etc., we've
lost three weeks out of the draughting room. The Prices are
welcome anytime now. Our best to you all.

Faithfully,

Frank Lloyd Wright

December 11th, 1952

TALIESIN WEST

---

70. Selected Correspondence (mainly Frank Lloyd Wright to Harold C. Price, Sr.) 1952-1959
Various media
8-1/2 x 11
Price Tower Arts Center
Gift of Harold C. Price Jr. 2004.02.01 - 2004.02.72

Exhibitions: Wichita, KS (2005, a similar example).
Selected References: none

CHRONOLOGICAL SELECTED BIBLIOGRAPHY

Wright, Frank Lloyd. "Frank Lloyd Wright." **Architectural Forum** 58 (January 1938): special issue 1-102.

Hitchcock, Henry-Russell. **In the Nature of Materials**. New York: Sloan and Pearce Duell, 1942.

Wright, Frank Lloyd. "Frank Lloyd Wright." **Architectural Forum** 88 (January 1948): 54, 65-156.

H.C. Price Company. **The Tie-In Quarterly** (March 1953): 1-3, 28.

"Frank Lloyd Wright's Concrete and Copper Skyscraper on the Prairie for H. C. Price Co." **Architectural Forum** 98 (May 1953): 98-105.

"Prairie Skyscraper." **Time** 61 (25 May 1953): 43.

"Tower to Provide Office, Living Space." **Engineering News-Record** (4 June 1953): 23.

"Price Tower Will Be Built in Bartlesville." **Construction News Monthly** (10 June 1953): 117-18.

Thomas, Mark. "F. L. W. Again," **Arch Design** (December 1953): 347-49.

"18-Story Tower Cantilever Structure of Concrete and Glass: Dramatic Frank Lloyd Wright Design." **Building Materials Digest** 14 (December 1954): 425.

Kaufmann, Jr., Edgar. **An American Architecture**. New York: Horizon Press, 1955.

Wright, Frank Lloyd. **The Story of the Tower: The Tree That Escaped the Crowded Forest**. New York: Horizon Press, 1956, reprinted in Bruce Brooks Pfeiffer, ed., **Frank Lloyd Wright: Collected Writings** Vol. 5 (1949-1959). New York: Rizzoli, 1995. 145-154.

"Frank Lloyd Wright: After 36 Years His Tower is Completed." **Architectural Forum** 104 (February 1956): 106-113.

"The H. C. Price Tower." **Architectural Record** 119 (February 1956): 153-160.

"Wright Completes Skyscraper." **Progressive Architecture** 37 (February 1956): 87-90.

"Frank Lloyd Wright; la 'Price Tower'." **Casabella Continuità** 211 (June-July 1956): 8-21.

"Een Amerikaans architectenbureau." **Bouw** [Rotterdam] 11, no. 31 (4 August 1956): 670-673.

"Gratte-ciel à Bartlesville, cité de 25,000 habitants, U.S.A." **Architecture d'aujourd'hui** 27 (October 1956): 23.

"The Lighting in Frank Lloyd Wright's Ultra Modern Tower." **Lighting** (December 1956): 26-27.

Wright, Frank Lloyd. **The Living City**. New York: Horizon Press, 1958.

Samona, Giuseppe, *et al*, **Drawings for a Living Architecture**. New York: Horizon Press, 1959.

Blake, Peter. **The Master Builders**. New York: W.W. Norton, 1960. 403-6.
Scully, Jr., Vincent. **Frank Lloyd Wright**. New York: George Braziller, 1960. 25-26.

Drexler, Arthur, ed. **The Drawings of Frank Lloyd Wright**. New York: Horizon Press for The Museum of Modern Art, 1962. 249-250, 313.

Futagawa, Yukio, and Martin Pawley, eds. **Frank Lloyd Wright: Public Buildings**. New York: Simon and Schuster, 1970. 18, 61-68, 122.

Izzo, Alberto, and Camillo Gubitossi, eds. **Designs 1887-1959**. Florence: Centro-Di, 1976.

Wright, Olgivanna Lloyd. **Selected Drawings** Portfolio Vol. I. Tokyo: A.D.A. Edita Tokyo Co. Ltd., 1977.

Hanks, David A. **The Decorative Designs of Frank Lloyd Wright**. New York: E. P. Dutton, 1979. 165-68.

Twombly, Robert C. **Frank Lloyd Wright: His Life and his Architecture**. New York: John Wiley and Sons, 1979. 350, 354-56, 413-15.

Wright, Olgivanna Lloyd. **Selected Drawings** Portfolio Vol. II. Tokyo: A.D.A. Edita Tokyo Co. Ltd., 1979.

De Long, David G. "A Tower Expressive of Unique Interiors." **AIA Journal** 71 (July 1982): 78-83.

Wright, Olgivanna Lloyd. **Selected Drawings** Portfolio Vol. III. Tokyo: A.D.A. Edita Tokyo Co. Ltd., 1982.

"Frank Lloyd Wright's Price Tower Wins AIA Twenty-five Year Award." **Architectural Record** 171 (April 1983): 83.

Futagawa, Yukio, and Bruce Brooks Pfeiffer, eds., **Frank Lloyd Wright in His Renderings 1887-1959**. Tokyo: A.D.A. Edita, 1984. 169.

Meehan, Patrick J., ed. **The Master Architect: Conversations with Frank Lloyd Wright**. New York: John Wiley & Sons, 1984. 23, 114, 135, 146, 147-151, 209, 237.

Pfeiffer, Bruce Brooks, ed., Yukio Futagawa, photographer. **Frank Lloyd Wright Monograph** Vol. 12. Tokyo: A.D.A. Edita Tokyo Co. Ltd., 1984.

Pfeiffer, Bruce Brooks, ed. **Preliminary Studies 1: 1889-1916**. Tokyo: A.D.A. Edita Tokyo Co. Ltd., 1985.

Pfeiffer, Bruce Brooks, ed., Yukio Futagawa, photographer. **Frank Lloyd Wright Monograph** Vol. 5: 1924-36. Tokyo: A.D.A. Edita Tokyo Co. Ltd., 1985.

Pfeiffer, Bruce Brooks. **Treasures of Taliesin, 76 Unbuilt Designs**. Fresno: The Press at California State University, and Carbondale: Southern Illinois University Press, 1985.

Wright, Frank Lloyd, and Frank Lloyd Wright Foundation. **Schumacher Drawings, Textile Patterns**. Flagstaff: Frank Lloyd Wright Foundation, 1985.

Doremus, Thomas. **Frank Lloyd Wright and Le Corbusier: The Great Dialogue**. New York: Van Nostrand Reinhold, 1985. 86, 143, 147, 162.

Pfeiffer, Bruce Brooks, ed. **Preliminary Studies 2: 1917-1932**. Tokyo: A.D.A. Edita Tokyo Co. Ltd., 1986.

Pfeiffer, Bruce Brooks, ed., Yukio Futagawa, photographer. **Frank Lloyd Wright Monograph** Vol. 6: 1937-41. Tokyo: A.D.A. Edita Tokyo Co. Ltd., 1986.

Lipman, Jonathan. **Frank Lloyd Wright and the Johnson Wax Buildings**. New York: Rizzoli, 1986.

Pfeiffer, Bruce Brooks, ed. **Frank Lloyd Wright: Letters to Clients**. Fresno: The Press at California State University, 1986. 291-302.

Futagawa, Yukio, and Bruce Brooks Pfeiffer, eds. **Frank Lloyd Wright: Preliminary Studies 3: 1933-1959**. Tokyo: A.D.A. Edita, 1987. 192-197.

Gill, Brendan. **Many Masks: A Life of Frank Lloyd Wright**. New York: G.P. Putnam's Sons, 1987. 423, 452-460.

Meehan, Patrick J., ed. **Truth Against the World: Frank Lloyd Wright Speaks for an Organic Architecture**. New York: John Wiley & Sons, 1987. 83, 105, 107.

Pfeiffer, Bruce Brooks, ed., Yukio Futagawa, photographer. **Frank Lloyd Wright Monograph** Vol. 7: 1942-1950. Tokyo: A.D.A. Edita Tokyo Co. Ltd., 1988.

Pfeiffer, Bruce Brooks, ed., Yukio Futagawa, photographer. **Frank Lloyd Wright Monograph** Vol. 8: 1951-1959. Tokyo: A.D.A. Edita, 1988. 64-71.

Wright, Frank Lloyd, and Bruce Brooks Pfeiffe. **Frank Lloyd Wright in the Realm of Ideas**. Carbondale: South Illinois University Press, 1988.

Hanks, David A. **Frank Lloyd Wright: Preserving An Architectural Heritage**. New York: F.P. Dutton 1989. 118 -119.

Pfeiffer, Bruce Brooks. **Frank Lloyd Wright Drawings: Masterworks from the Frank Lloyd Wright Archives**. New York: Harry N. Abrams, 1990. 120-121.

Pfeiffer, Bruce Brooks. **Frank Lloyd Wright Drawings**. New York: Harry Abrams, 1990.

Massu, Claude. **Frank Lloyd Wright**. Paris: Pierre Trincal, 1990.

McCarter, Robert, ed. **Frank Lloyd Wright: A Primer on Architectural Principles**. New York: Princeton Architectural Press, 1991. 280.

Fuller, R. Buckminster, in Patrick J. Meehan, ed., **Frank Lloyd Wright Remembered**: Washington, D.C.: Preservation Press, 1991. 40-41.

Pfeiffer, Bruce Brooks. **Frank Lloyd Wright**. Koln: Taschen, 1991.

Wright, Frank Lloyd, and Frank Lloyd Wright Foundation. **The Designs of Frank Lloyd Wright, Owned by the Frank Lloyd Wright Foundation**. Flagstaff: Frank Lloyd Wright Foundation, 1991.

Lipman, Jonathan and Kisho Kurokawa. **Frank Lloyd Wright Retrospective**. Nagano: Mainichi Newspaper, 1991.

Laseau, Paul, and James Tice. **Frank Lloyd Wright: Between Principle and Form**. New York: Van Nostrand Reinhold, 1992. 148-49.

Apostolo, Roberto. "La Price Tower di Frank Lloyd Wright," **Frames, Porte & Finestre** (August-September 1992): 54-61.

Wright, Frank Lloyd, and Bruce Brooks Pfeiffer. **Frank Lloyd Wright Collected Writings** Vol. 2. New York: Rizzoli, 1992.

Storrer, William A. **The Frank Lloyd Wright Companion**. Chicago: University of Chicago Press, 1993. 378-79.

Hart, Spencer. **Frank Lloyd Wright**. Greenwich, Conn.: Barnes & Noble, Inc., 1993. 24 -25.

Wright, Frank Lloyd, and Bruce Brooks Pfeiffer. **Frank Lloyd Wright Collected Writings** Vol. 3. New York: Rizzoli, 1993.

Heinz, Thomas A. **Frank Lloyd Wright Interiors and Furniture**. London: Academy Editions, 1994. 212.

Patterson, Terry L. **Frank Lloyd Wright and the Meaning of Materials**. New York: Van Nostrand Reinhold, 1994. 164-65, 167, 168, 178, 200, 201, 218.

Cover of **The Tie-In Quarterly**, the H.C. Price Company publication, with the Price Tower rendering. Gift of Izola Moore (PTAC 2001.02).

Price Tower at night. Photograph by Joe Price (PTAC 2004.15.02).

Etlin, Richard. **Frank Lloyd Wright and Le Corbusier: The Romantic Legacy**. Manchester and New York: Manchester University Press, 1994. 62-63.

Wright, Frank Lloyd, and Bruce Brooks Pfeiffer. **Frank Lloyd Wright Collected Writings** Vol. 4. New York: Rizzoli, 1994.

Riley, Terence, and Peter Reed eds. **Frank Lloyd Wright: Architect**. New York: The Museum of Modern Art, 1994. 52, 70, 281, 290-92.

Hertz, David M. **Frank Lloyd Wright in Word and Form**. New York: G.K. Hall, 1995. 111-12.

Wright, Frank Lloyd, and Bruce Brooks Pfeiffer. **Frank Lloyd Wright Collected Writings** Vol. 5. New York: Rizzoli, 1995.

Besinger, Curtis. **Working With Mr. Wright: What It Was Like**. New York: Cambridge University Press, 1997. 242-43, 247, 249, 262, 270, 283-84.

Thompson, Iain. **Frank Lloyd Wright**. Berkeley: Thunder Bay press, Inc., 1997. 17, 164-165.

Eaton, Timothy A. ed. **Frank Lloyd Wright The Seat of Genius: Chairs 1895- 1955**. West Palm Beach: Eaton Fine Art, Inc, 1997. 64, 65.

McCarter, Robert. **Frank Lloyd Wright**. London: Phaidon Press, 1997. 198-200.

Wright, Frank Lloyd, and Edgar Kaufmann, Jr. **An American Architecture**. New York: Barnes and Noble Books, 1998.

De Long, David G. ed. **Frank Lloyd Wright and the Living City**. Milan: Skira, 1998.120.

Hoffmann, Donald. **Frank Lloyd Wright, Louis Sullivan, and the Skyscraper**. New York: Dover, 1998. 71-81.

Thompson, Iain. **Frank Lloyd Wright: A Visual Encyclopedia**. London: PRC Publishing Ltd., 1999. 266.

Pfeiffer, Bruce Brooks. **Treasures of Taliesin, 77 Unbuilt Designs**. San Francisco: Pomegranate, 1999.

Lucas, Suzette, ed. **Frank Lloyd Wright Quarterly** Vol. 12, No. 1 (Winter 2001): 28.

Storrer, William Allin. **The Architecture of Frank Lloyd Wright: A Complete Catalogue**, 3rd ed. Chicago: University of Chicago Press, 2002. 359.

Kellogg, Craig. "Matter of Design: Full Time Job," **Interior Design** (New York: Reed Business Information, July 2003): 174 -175.

Dillon, David. "The Inn at Price Tower," **Architectural Record** (New York: McGraw-Hill Companies, July 2003): 118 -125.

Abel, Chris. **Sky High: Vertical Architecture**. Vincenza: Graphicom, 2003. 26.

Futagawa, Yukio, and Bruce Brooks Pfeiffer. **GA Travelers: Frank Lloyd Wright Architecture**. Tokyo: A.D.A. Edita Tokyo Co., Ltd., 2003. 160-183.

Schmertz, Mildred F. "Inn at Price Tower: An Oklahoma Hotel Finds a Home in Frank Lloyd Wright's 1950s High-Rise," **Architectural Digest** (New York: Conde Nast Publications, June 2003): 72, 74, 76, 77.

ON THE REHABILITATION

Guise, David. "Preservation: Price Tower Vacant." **Progressive Architecture** 70 (April 1989): 21, 26.

Ricapito, Maria. "The Tree That Escaped the Forest." **Metropolis** 17 (February-March 1998): 52.

"Price Tower 45th Anniversary Celebration and Fundraising Campaign Announced." **Frank Lloyd Wright Quarterly** 12 (Winter 2001): 28.

Holzman, Anna. "Rooms at the Wright Price. **Architecture** 91 (November 2002): 17.

Dillon, David. "Wendy Evans Joseph Turns an Iconic Work by Frank Lloyd Wright into the Inn at Price Tower with No Edginess Lost." **Architectural Record** 191 (July 2003): 118-24.

Kellogg, Craig. "Full-Job: It's No Easy Task Restoring the Executive Quarters at Frank Lloyd Wright's Price Tower in Oklahoma." **Interior Design** 74 (July 2003): 174-75.

Gladstone, Valerie. "Stone Walls and Copper Veils." **Art News** 102 (November 2003): 92.

FOR FURTHER REFERENCE

Moholy-Nagy, Sibyl. **College Art Journal**, Vol. 18, No. 4. (Summer, 1959): 319-329, 324-25.

Mather, E. Cotton. "On the American Great Plains" **Annals of the Association of American Geographers**, Vol. 62, No. 2. (Jun., 1972): 237-257; 248-51.

Brown, Patricia Leigh. "Built on Oil, Banking on Design." **New York Times**, 16 October 2003, F1.

Wright, Frank Lloyd. **A Testament**. New York: Horizon Press, 1957.

EXHIBITIONS

Frank Lloyd Wright: European Tour, Amsterdam, Holland, Brussels, Antwerp, Belgium, Berlin, Germany, 1931.

Frank Lloyd Wright, Museum of Modern Art, New York, NY, 1941.

Frank Lloyd Wright, Sixty Years of Living Architecture, Florence, Italy / Zurich, Switzerland / Paris, France / Rotterdam, Netherlands, 1951-1954 and Frank Lloyd Wright, Sixty Years of Living Architecture, Mexico City, Mexico / New York, NY / Los Angeles, CA, 1951-1954.

Frank Lloyd Wright, Museum of Modern Art, New York, NY, 1962.

Day at Taliesin, Seminars, Taliesin, Spring Green, WI / Taliesin West, Scottsdale, AZ, 1980-1988.

Frank Lloyd Wright, Drawings, Masterworks from the Archives, Phoenix Art Museum, Phoenix, AZ, 1990.

The Tree That Escaped the Crowded Forest, The Bartlesville Museum (now Price Tower Arts Center), Bartlesville, OK. 1990.

The Right Site; Wright in Wisconsin, Milwaukee Art Museum, Milwaukee, WI, 1992.

Frank Lloyd Wright: Architect, Museum of Modern Art, New York, NY, 1994.

Les Annees 30, Paris, Palais de Chaillot, France, 1997.

At the End of the Century: 100 Years of Architecture, Tokyo, Cologne, Mexico City, Chicago, Los Angeles, 1998-2000.

Frank Lloyd Wright: The Vertical Dimension, The Skyscraper Museum, New York, NY, 2004.

Historical Frank Lloyd Wright Objects On Display, Wichita Art Museum, KS, 2005.

Note: The drawings referred to in the text are from the collection of the Frank Lloyd Wright Foundation, Scottsdale, AZ, and are notated with the Foundation's archival number.

ABBREVIATIONS

FLW	Frank Lloyd Wright
FLWA	Frank Lloyd Wright Archives, Taliesin West, Scottsdale, Arizona
HCPJr	Harold C. Price, Jr.
HCPSr	Harold C. Price, Sr.
JSAH	Journal of the Society of Architectural Historians
LPC-OHA	Landmark Preservation Council Oral History Archive, Bartlesville, Oklahoma
PTAC	Price Tower Arts Center Archives

1 Frank Lloyd Wright to Harold C. Price, Jr., (subsequently referred to as FLW and HCPJr, respectively), 26 May1952. Price Tower Arts Center (subsequently referred to as PTAC) 2004.02.01.

2 Harold C. Price, Sr., (subsequently referred to as HCPSr) to FLW, 16 June 1952. All documents in the archives of the Frank Lloyd Wright Foundation, Scottsdale, Arizona are identified by the acronym FLWA.

3 E.L. Gallery to FLW, 24 July 1952. FLWA.

4 HCPSr to FLW, 19 August 1952. FLWA.

5 FLW to HCPSr, 16 September 1952. PTAC 2004.02.05.

6 FLW to HCPSr, 26 September 1952. PTAC 2004.02.06.

7 HCPSr to FLW, 27 October 1952. FLWA.

8 FLW to HCPSr, 4 November 1952. PTAC 2004.02.07.

9 FLW to HCPSr, 11 December 1952. PTAC 2004.02.08.

10 HCPSr to FLW, 2 January 1953. PTAC 2004.02.11.

11 HCPSr to FLW, 12 March 1953. FLWA.

12 HCPSr to FLW, 2 April 1953. FLWA.

13 HCPSr to FLW, 6 April 1953. FLWA.

14 FLW to HCPSr, 17 April 1953. PTAC 2004.02.13.

15 FLW to HCPSr, 18 April 1953. PTAC 2004.02.14.

16 Script by FLW, 17 April 1953. PTAC 2004.02.15.

17 HCPSr to FLW, 20 April 1953. FLWA.

18 HCPSr to FLW, 30 April 1953. FLWA.

19 HCPSr to FLW, 11 May 1953. PTAC 2004.02.20.

20 HCPSr to FLW, 12 March 1953. FLWA.

21 FLW to HCPSr, 19 May 1953. PTAC 2004.02.21.

22 FLW to HCPSr, 4 June 1953. PTAC 2004.02.24.

23 HCPSr to FLW, 5 June 1953. PTAC 2004.02.25.

24 HCPSr to FLW, 8 June 1953. PTAC 2004.02.226.

25 4 July 1953, FLWF 5215.094, 5214.042, 5215.069, 5215.070, 5215.076, 5215.057, 5215.055.

26 HCPSr to FLW, 13 July 1953. Joe Price, in discussion with the author, October 2004, recalled window frames were originally specified by Wright to be bronze who later specified aluminum in order to build the tower.

27 E.L. Gallery to FLW, 14 July 1953. FLWA.

28 Samuel R. Lewis to Mr. Glickman, 22 July 1953. FLWA.

29 E.L. Gallery to FLW, 30 July 1953. FLWA.

30 24 August 1953. FLWF 5215.062, 5125.064, 5215.066, 5215.089, 5215.092.

31 28 October 1953. FLWF 5215.081, 5215.048.

32 HCPSr to FLW, 24 November 1953. FLWA.

33 HCPSr to FLW, 22 October 1954. FLWA. In this October letter, Price, Sr. brings to Wright's attention the fact that he last visited the building in January.

34 Joe Price to FLW, 18 January 1954. FLWA.

35 William Wesley Peters to Huskell Cullwell, 25 January 1954. FLWF 5251.044, 521.062.

36 William Wesley Peters to HCPJr, 24 February 1954. FLWA.

37 HCPSr to FLW, 13 March 1954. FLWA.

38 HCPSr to FLW, 17 May 1954. FLWA.

39 HCPJr to FLW, 12 April 1954. FLWA.

40 Haskell Culwell to FLW, 18 May 1954. FLWA.

41 E.L. Gallery to FLW, 26 August 1954. FLWA.

42 Haskell Culwell to Industiral Electric Company, 1 October 1954. FLWA.

43 HCPSr to FLW, 22 October 1954. FLWA.

44 HCPSr to FLW, 4 December 1954. PTAC 2004.02.43.

45 HCPSr to FLW, 15 January 1955. FLWA.

46 Haskell Culwell to FLW, 14 February 1955. FLWA.

47 William Wesley Peters to Haskell Culwell, 12 April 1955. FLWA.

48 HCPSr to FLW, 25 May 1955. FLWA.

49 Mary Lou Price to FLW, 5 June 1955. FLWA.

50 FLW to Joe Price, 7 June 1955. FLWA.

51 HCPSr to FLW, 22 June 1954. FLWA.

52 Joe Price to FLW, 10 August 1955. FLWF.

53 HCPSr to FLW, 20 August 1955. FLWA.

54 HCPSr to FLW, 2 September 1955. FLWA.

55 Joe Price to Eugene Masselink, 21 September 1955. FLWA.

56 Joe Price to FLW, 21 September 1955. FLWA.

57 Conversation with Joe Price, at the Price Tower Arts Center, September 2004.

58 HCPSr to Jeanne Davers, Associate Editor, 30 September 1955. FLWA.

59 E.L. Gallery to HCPSr, 16 November 1955. FLWA.

60 Joe Price to FLW, 18 November 1955. FLWA.

61 Spinning Wheel Rug to Joe Price, 21 December 1955. FLWA.

62 Joe Price to Eugene Masselink, 22 December 1955. FLWA.

63 HCPSr to FLW, 27 December 1955. FLWA.

64 FLW to HCPSr, 28 December 1955. FLWA.

65 Joe Price to FLW, 2 January 1956. FLWA.

66 Joe Price to FLW, 19 January 1956. FLWA.

67 FLW to HCPSr, 4 February 1956. PTAC 2004.02.52a.

68 *The Bartlesville Advertiser* (newspaper front page and central article), February 9, 1956.

69 FLW to HCPSr, 29 February 1956. PTAC 2004.02.53.

70 FLW to HCPSr, 22 February 1956. FLWA.

71 HCPSr to Elliot V. Bell, Editor and Publisher of *Business Week*, 23 February 1956. FLWA.

72 K.S. Adams (Chairman of Phillips Petroleum Company) to HCPSr, 3 May 1956. PTAC 2004.02.56.

73 HCPSr to K.S. Adams, 4 May 1956. PTAC 2004.02.57.

74 HCPSr to FLW, 4 May 1956. PTAC 2004.02.58.

75 HCPSr to FLW, 5 July 1956. FLWA.

76 FLW to HCPSr, 2 July 1956. PTAC 2004.02.60.

77 HCPSr to FLW, 11 December 1956. FLWA.

78 Joe Price to FLW, 17 December 1956. FLWA.

79 Henry Bass to HCPSr, 21 March 1957. FLWA.

80 Olgivanna Lloyd Wright to the Prices, 16 March 1959. PTAC 2004.02.78.

81 John Calvin Womack, *A Report on Floors 17,18 and 19*, NEA#0342006019, 2004. P. 10.

82 Phillips Petroleum Company, News release, 17 December 1980.

83 The American Institute of Architects, Press release, Washington D.C., 1 March 1983.

84 PTAC archives from Landmark Preservation Council.

85 PTAC archives from Landmark Preservation Council.

86 John Calvin Womak, *A Report on Floors 17,18 and 19*, NEA#0342006019, 2004 John Womack Report. P. 10.

View of the exterior patinated copper panels and louvers. Photograph by Christian M Korab / Korab Photo, 2004.

NOTES ON CONTRIBUTORS

Anthony Alofsin is Roland Roessner Centennial Professor of Architecture and Professor of Art and Art History at the University of Texas at Austin. Author, lecturer, designer, he has written extensively on Frank Lloyd Wright and modern architecture. His five-volume *Frank Lloyd Wright: An Index to the Taliesin Correspondence* (Garland, 1988) won the Vasari Award in 1989 and opened a new era in scholarly research on Wright. His book *Frank Lloyd Wright: The Lost Years, 1910-1922* (Chicago, 1993) defined a previously undocumented phase of Wright's life and work. He was Consulting Curator of "Frank Lloyd Wright, Architect," the major retrospective exhibition held at the Museum of Modern Art, New York in 1994. His books on modern architecture include *The Struggle for Modernism: Architecture, Landscape Architecture, and City Planning at Harvard* (W.W. Norton, 2002) and *Architecture and Language in the Habsburg Empire and Its Successor States, 1867-1933* (University of Chicago Press, 2005). He writes review essays for the *Times Literary Supplement*, and is currently editing a book of essays on I.M. Pei's East Building for the National Gallery of Art, Washington, DC.

Hilary Ballon is Professor in the Department of Art History and Archaeology at Columbia University. Her essay in this volume is based on her forthcoming book, *Frank Lloyd Wright's Towers* (forthcoming from W.W. Norton). She has also curated "Frank Lloyd Wright: The Vertical Dimension (2004-05)," which brought together all of Wrights highrise projects. Ballon's earlier publications include *The Paris of Henri IV: Architecture and Urbanism*, *Louis Le Vau: Mazarin's College*, *Colbert's Revenge*, and *New York's Pennsylvania Stations*.

Pat Kirkham is Professor of Design History at the Bard Graduate Center for Studies in the Decorative Arts, Design, and Culture, New York. She has written widely on design, gender, and film. Her work on furniture and interiors covers the eighteenth, nineteenth and twentieth centuries. Her best known publications include *Charles and Ray Eames: Designers of the Twentieth Century* (MIT Press, 1995), *Women Designers in the USA, 1900-2000: Diversity and Difference* (editor and contributor, and curator of the eponymous exhibition, Yale University Press/BGC, 2000), *The Gendered Object* (ed. Manchester University Press, 1996), and *A View from The Interior* (ed. with Judith Attfield, The Women's Press, 1989 and 1995). Her latest book is *Saul Bass: A Life in Design and Film, Elaine Bass: A Collaboration in Film and Life* (Laurence King, in press, 2005) and her current project (with Sarah Lichtman) is *Twentieth Century Interiors* (Laurence King, forthcoming).

Mónica Ramírez-Montagut is Curator of Collections and Public Programs at Price Tower Arts Center. She received her degree in architecture from the Universidad Iberoamericana (UIA), Mexico. She then pursued postgraduate studies in the theory and history of architecture at the Universitat Politécnica de Catalunya (UPC) in Barcelona, Spain, from which she received her master's and her Ph.D. with a cum laude dissertation on *Marcel Broodthaers: His Museum*. She has lectured widely on this subject, using it to illuminate the relationship between contemporary art and its institutional context. In the field of contemporary art, Ramírez-Montagut has served as Assistant Curator at the Aldrich Contemporary Art Museum in Connecticut, also worked as an independent curator in New York City organizing a number of exhibitions of emerging Latino artists and she was Program Coordinator for the *Mexico Now* festival, organized by Arts International Inc., New York.

Scott W. Perkins is a PhD Candidate at the Bard Graduate Center for Studies in the Decorative Arts, Design, and Culture in New York, where he completed his MA in 2003. His interests are primarily the architecture, interiors, and decorative arts of the nineteenth and twentieth centuries. While a student at the School of the Art Institute of Chicago, he documented the furniture and decorative arts of Wright's Taliesin East estate in Spring Green. A practicing interior designer, he is also an adjunct Critical Studies instructor at Parsons School of Design/New School University, New York.

Joseph M. Siry has taught the history of modern architecture and urbanism in the Department of Art and Art History at Wesleyan University since 1984. His books are *Carson Pirie Scott: Louis Sullivan and the Chicago Department Store* (University of Chicago Press, 1988), *Unity Temple: Frank Lloyd Wright and Architecture for Liberal Religion* (Cambridge University Press, 1996), and *The Chicago Auditorium Building: Adler and Sullivan's Architecture and the City* (University of Chicago Press, 2002). This last book won the 2003 Alice Davis Hitchcock Award from the Society of Architectural Historians for the best book by a North American scholar published in 2002. He has published articles on Adler and Sullivan, and Wright, in the *Journal of the Society of Architectural Historians*. An article on Wright's Unity Temple won the College Art Association's Arthur Kingsley Porter Prize for the best article by a younger scholar in the Art Bulletin in 1991. He is currently working on a book on Wright's later public architecture.